THE
EDIBLE
MUSHROOM

◇ ◇ ◇

THE
EDIBLE
MUSHROOM

A Gourmet Cook's Guide

MARGARET LEIBENSTEIN

Illustrations by Monika Bittman

FAWCETT COLUMBINE ◇ NEW YORK

A Fawcett Columbine Book
Published by Ballantine Books
Copyright © 1986 by Margaret Leibenstein
Illustrations copyright © 1986 by Monika Bittman

The author is grateful for permission to include the following recipes:
Paula Wolfert's Asparagus with Black Morels. Copyright © 1985 by Paula
Wolfert. *Sauté of Snails and Boletes.* Copyright © 1985 by L'Academie
de Cuisine, Inc., François M. Dionot. *Stewed Chanterelles in Ginger
Sauce.* Copyright © 1985 by Julie Sahni. *The Romagnolis' Pasta with
Porcini and Tomato Sauce.* Copyright © 1985 by Margaret and G.
Franco Romagnoli. *Stir-fried Rainbow Vegetables in a Spicy Ginger-Garlic
Sauce.* Copyright © 1984 by Nina Simonds.

LIBRARY OF CONGRESS CATALOGING-IN-PUBLICATION DATA

Leibenstein, Margaret.
    The edible mushroom.

    Includes index.
    1. Cookery (Mushrooms)   2. Mushrooms, Edible.
I. Title.
TX804.L45   1986   641.6'58   86-90740
ISBN 0-449-90204-8

Text Design by Mary A. Wirth
Cover painting by Monika Bittman

Manufactured in the United States of America
First Edition: October 1986
10 9 8 7 6 5 4 3 2 1

◇   ◇   ◇

TO
HARVEY

◇ ◇ ◇

CONTENTS

◇   ◇   ◇

RECIPES

◇ ◇ ◇

ACKNOWLEDGMENTS

No cookbook is the product of a single effort. Without the assistance and encouragement of Professor Donald H. Pfister, Director of the Farlow Herbarium, and Geraldine C. Kaye, Librarian of the Farlow Library, both of Harvard University, I could have neither begun nor completed this project.

Don Pfister patiently examined each mushroom I brought him and taught me to trust my nose and sense of touch when determining their freshness. Lessons that proved invaluable.

My deepest debt of gratitude is to Gerry Kaye, who guided my first faltering steps through a confusing maze of mycological nomenclature, then, figuratively, held my hand as I began my solitary forays through the immense literature associated with mushrooms. As the book progressed, she constantly kept me informed of new developments in both the scientific and popular literature. Happily, our relationship, which began as "strictly intellectual business," has grown into a warm and cherished friendship.

I am grateful to my fellow members of the Culinary Historians of Boston, notably Bonnie Brown, Sheryl Julian,

Sonia Landes, Lottie Mendelsohn, Cynthia Rubin, Joyce Toomre, and, of course, Barbara Wheaton, for their suggestions, bibliographical data, and encouragement; and to my colleagues in the Women's Culinary Guild of New England who gave me the opportunity to mount a major mushroom tasting for them. Their questions and enthusiasms helped in the organization of the final manuscript. I am indebted to the fine cooking professionals who kindly contributed those recipes you will find attributed to them. In addition, I would like to thank two extremely talented young chefs, Lydia Shire and Moncef Meddeb of Boston, who though unable to develop new recipes for the book because of their demanding schedules, were very generous with advice and information.

Many friends here and abroad offered anecdotes, advice, and recipe suggestions. Alan and Jane Davidson, Charles and Ann Korvin, Dr. Jurg and Freni Egger, Dino and Eva Sonnino, the late novelist Irwin Shaw and his lovely wife Marian, Barbara and Fredi Morel, Alexander de Beer, Bibi Bentzel, and the Libnics of Mexico City and California, all in their own way contributed to the successful completion of this book.

Professor Moselio Schaechter, Chairman of the Department of Molecular Biology and Microbiology at Tufts University Medical School, answered my questions with patience, expertise and exceptional good humor, and Professor Yori Oda of Harvard University was of unparalleled help in untangling the intricacies of certain Japanese terms. Barbara Haber, Elisabeth Shenton, and the other staff members of the Schlesinger Library of Radcliffe College made research a pleasurable and rewarding activity. Felicia Eth and Ann Edelstein, my agents, encouraged, guided, and smoothed the process from concept to completion; while Virginia Faber, my editor, good naturedly questioned, corrected, and kept me to deadline. My thanks to all.

My good friends and neighbors Elisabeth Bishop and Joan Kleinman, whose advice and support I could not have done without, deserve special mention, as do Alan Warner and Pia Jacobsen of Le Jardin of Cambridge, Massachusetts, and John Hines of the Northwest Mushroom Co. of Portland, Oregon, for making available a ready supply of the mushrooms required to test those recipes that eventually made it into the book and the many more that did not.

Yet with all the help given, this book would have remained stillborn had it not been for the never-failing love, humor, support, and sacrifice of my husband, Harvey Leibenstein. He reassured me when I doubted; made me smile when I was dejected; reminded me of file copies when the computer failed; and ate everything put in front of him with a constructively critical palate. Greater love hath no man than to give up a 34-inch waistline for his wife. Harvey, for everything I thank you.

—Margaret Leibenstein
Cambridge, Massachusetts

◇   ◇   ◇

INTRODUCTION

Mushrooms have delighted, mystified, and fed man from the dawn of time. When our earliest ancestors hunted animals for a living, they also gathered the fungi which sprang up, seemingly from nowhere, all around them in the forests. But "the wild" was an uncertain food provisioner and so early man began to domesticate animals to provide a sure food source. Little by little mankind's entire food supply has come under some form of domestication or cultivation.

The last of man's edibles to succumb have been the fungi, and of those only a few varieties have been encouraged to grow outside of their natural habitats, so we are still pretty much dependent on nature to meet our demand for these savory esculents.

To indulge a craving for caviar you need only find a specialty store that sells the expensive stuff. Mushrooms, however, have their seasons. A craving for fresh morels can only be satisfied in spring. If your appetite runs to fresh cepes you will have to wait until late spring or early fall. For that reason this book is arranged by growing seasons.

A DIFFERENT KIND OF GUIDE

Unlike other guides to wild mushrooms, this one will not send you scurrying for them under oak trees or in pine forests. I suggest instead that you look next to the radicchio or baby zucchinis in your favorite specialty store or supermarket. This is a guide for culinary adventurers who prefer their palatal experiments approved by the FDA or, at least, monitored by the public health department—for urban and suburban cooks who enjoy using exciting ingredients to create novel and distinctive dishes.

First, you'll find a short history of edible mushrooms and some general rules for buying, washing, preparing, and preserving mushrooms.

The remainder of the book is arranged by season and contains information and tempting recipes for that season's crop of mushrooms. Most mushrooms found in markets in this country come from the West Coast and Pacific Northwest, so seasonal designations are based on when mushrooms appear in those regions. In the spring you will find morels and boletes. The largest number of species appears in late summer through fall. In winter the treasured truffles appear. A final brief section covers the treatment of and recipes for dried varieties, which are, of course, available all year round. In addition, you will find favorite recipes from some of America's finest chefs and food writers to show you how professionals use these exciting ingredients.

It is lots of fun to shop for, cook with, and eat wild mushrooms but, for me, their greatest value is in their ability to enrich our sensibilities. Coming upon a basket of boletes or chanterelles alongside, say, the carrots we have come to take for granted, cannot fail to conjure up a vision of nature's power, beauty, and unpredictability. Because their flavors dramatically change every dish to which they are added, wild mushrooms produce an almost primeval response that reminds us that food is a source of sensual pleasure, not just nourishment. If mushrooms do nothing more than that they are worth their weight in gold.

◇　◇　◇

MUSHROOMS
in HISTORY

As a child growing up in an essentially Anglo-Saxon culture, my feelings about mushrooms were mixed. I didn't associate my Polish grandmother's luscious soups with those strange earthly eruptions I had been warned not to touch at summer camp. Years later, living in Italy, I tasted my first wild mushroom out of the context of grandmother's rich barley and mushroom broth. That's all it took to teach me the enormous pleasures to be had from cooking and eating them. But I never attempted to pick mushrooms myself. The marketplace was my hunting ground. In spring the market stalls sported small straw baskets lined with young grape leaves on which the first morels of the season were lovingly displayed. As late summer and early fall rolled around, great willow and reed baskets filled almost to overflowing with boletes, chanterelles, meadow mushrooms, and many other species seemed to crowd out the other vegetables. With every purchase a bouquet of fresh herbs was thrust upon one.

Needless to say it was with some disappointment that I returned home to find that, while these same fungi grew in America, they could only be enjoyed by those with sufficient knowledge to pick them.

Happily, those days are over. Since the culinary dark ages of the 1950s Americans have become among the most sophisticated gastronomes in the world. We have expanded our gustatory horizons beyond all national, regional, and ethnic limits to the point where a truly cross-cultural cuisine is emerging as American. In some cities there is hardly an area of the world or a cultural group whose cuisine is not represented by a restaurant or cooking school. We have become culinary experimenters, cooking and pairing foods our parents would never have attempted. We are demanding and getting ingredients once considered exotic, available only in the most exclusive restaurants. Witness the now ubiquitous kiwi from New Zealand, jicama from Mexico, and uncounted varieties of chili peppers from Thailand. Perhaps the most exciting development has been the newfound appreciation of our native bounty—wild salad greens, blue cornmeal, native salmon, and especially edible wild mushrooms.

The mushroom craze is new in America but in most parts of the world the subtle flavors and earthy aromas of esculent fungi have delighted gourmets from time immemorial. Kings of ancient Babylon dined on quince-sized truffles from the African deserts. And one mushroom (the *Amanita caesarea*) pleased the Roman emperors so much that they named it the imperial fungus. Others like boletes (*Boletus edulis*), puffballs (*Lycoperdon*), and, of course, truffles, (*Tuber melanosporum* and *Tuber magnatum*) also commanded the Caesars' devotion. Historians still argue whether it was Caligula or the Emperor Claudius who proclaimed mushrooms "food of the gods"—too good for the common folk. Laws were passed forbidding ordinary citizens to eat them, while patrician Romans consumed as many mushrooms as they could afford.

Fungi were so highly prized that no mere servant was allowed to cook them. Roman aristocrats prepared all their own mushroom dishes in special silver vessels called "boleteria." Guests could tell where they stood in their host's esteem by the number and variety of mushroom dishes offered to them.

It was an age of affluence. Gracious living was translated

into spacious villas and lavish parties. Like all such times it spawned its share of handwringers and headshakers. Echoing the age-old despair over what the younger generation was coming to, Pliny, sometime in the first century A.D., wrote ". . . our fine-mouthed and daintie wantons . . . set such store by their tooth . . . [they] take great delight to dress this dish only with their own hands, that they may feed thereon in conceit and cogitation. . . ." Imagine toga-clad Yuppies going about "their business with their fine knives and razors of amber and other vessels of silver. . . ." Conceit and cogitation notwithstanding, there's no evidence that Pliny turned down any daintie wanton's invitation to dine. "I for my part," he confesses, "also am content to . . . accommodate myself to their humorous fancies. . . ."

The Latin love affair with edible fungi was not limited to the Romans. Pleasure-seeking Pompeians decorated their homes with frescoes depicting game and wild mushrooms. Nor would the Etruscans, whose sumptuous and frequent feasting moved the Romans to nickname them derisively *obesus* (or "fatsos"), have willingly passed up the delicacies of the fields and woods around them.

To this day the Italians are enthusiastic gatherers. In the spring and fall mushroom hunting becomes the occasion for large family picnics. Grandparents, parents, and children go off into the countryside, baskets and knives at the ready, in pursuit of esculent fungi. Picnic baskets full of pungent sausages, fragrant cheeses, fruit, crusty country breads, and, of course, wine are carried along and joyously devoured between forays. At the end of the day, every mushroom picked is carefully checked by the most knowledgeable member of the family, or by the official village mushroom "witch," and only the unquestionably edible ones are kept. For many Italians these outings are among the most treasured of childhood memories.

The same scene has been played out every year for generations and generations in France, Germany, Scandinavia, and most enthusiastically in Eastern Europe. Hungarians, who throughout their history have been sharply divided by religious, political, and ideological differences, are united in their adulation of wild mushrooms. Poles are passionate mycophiles and Russians respond physically, according to Vladimir Nabokov, to "that special boletic reek which makes a Russian's nostril dilate. . . ."

On the other hand, the attitude of English-speaking countries has been, until recently, reticent at best. But even though the English cannot be accused of being riotously enthusiastic about mushrooms, English cookbooks have historically included some recipes for their use. For example, in *The Forme of Cury,* a collection of recipes dating from 1390, there is a recipe for "Funges." The book we have come to know as Martha Washington's cookbook, *A Booke of Cookery,* which, according to Karen Hess, the eminent American culinary historian, was probably a sixteenth century English manuscript, contained a recipe "To Dress A Dish of Mushrumps," and a recipe "To Make the Pasty Royall," which called for "mushrumps." The eighteenth century English runaway best seller, *The Art of Cookery Made Plain and Easy* by Hannah Glasse, contains no less than 110 recipes that called for "mushrooms," "morels," or "truffles." While historians are bound to point out the clear French influence in English cookbooks, it is safe to assume that if the recipes were there, and continued to appear in subsequent editions, the English were eating mushrooms.

Asia is not immune to the lure of the fungus world. In

China the *Ling Chih,* "Fungus of Immortality," *(Ganoderma lucidum)* has been sought since the Han dynasty. It is believed to possess exceptional medicinal as well as aphrodisiac properties. The Chinese use over 100 varieties of wild mushrooms for medicinal purposes, and in cooking, innumerable varieties of fungi, only a very few of which are even known to Western cooks, play supporting roles in a seemingly infinite number of dishes.

Japanese cuisine makes abundant use of black mushrooms, which they call shiitake. But while the Japanese enjoy shiitakes, they *treasure* the matsutake. In autumn, when leaves in the forests have turned brilliant reds and golds, this thick-stemmed, handsome mushroom makes its appearance beneath large pine trees. Centuries ago hunting for them was the pastime of the nobility. And, as in all things Japanese, the hunt was governed by elaborate rules of dress, speech, and behavior. Today, because of changes in Japanese life-style, the matsutake is almost an endangered species. In order to meet the high consumer demand, they must be flown in from Korea and the United States, which adds considerably to their cost. A single fresh matsutake can cost between $40 and $60. Price, however, doesn't discourage the Japanese devotee. During the season market stalls are so filled with matsutakes that it is said that you can flavor your rice bowl with their scent just by strolling through the market. Unfortunately, unlike the shiitake, the flavor of the matsutake does not stand up well to drying. They must be eaten fresh, and attempts to cultivate the matsutake have so far proved unsuccessful.

◇   ◇   ◇

CULTIVATION—THE WAVE OF THE FUTURE

Mushrooms are exceptionally vulnerable to changes in season, temperature, and humidity. Furthermore, they are considered an unreliable food source because they do not necessarily appear in the same place or in the same quantities from year to year. For these reasons and because they must be hand-gathered, it is rare that they hold a central place in any cuisine. However, in the Far East, where Buddhism dictates vegetarianism, they share an important position in family and temple cooking with other alternative sources of protein. It is not unlikely that mushrooms were first cultivated in Southeast Asia.

No one knows how or why cultivation was started. Was it in response to demand or just serendipity? Did some woodsman simply notice that a log placed near another log on which shiitakes grew would yield more shiitakes? We'll never know. We do know that the Chinese were cultivating wood ear fungi in 300 B.C. and in Japan cultivation has been going on for at least 600 years. In Europe it developed much later.

As late as the mid-seventeenth century in England Dioscorides, the ancient Greek physician who served in Nero's army, was being quoted on how to "bring forth mushromes or toad-stools that are good to be eaten." By the beginning of the eighteenth century the French were describing a method for cultivating fungi in beds, and in 1731 the first English edition of *The Gardener's Dictionary* described ". . . the Method practis'd by the Gardeners who cultivate them for Sale" in the countryside around London. Hannah Glasse, in the third edition of her book, published in 1748, told her readers that on "Hot beds, Purslain, Cucumbers and Mushrooms" should be found. If we are to believe Mrs. Glasse, cultivated mushrooms were a staple crop in the kitchen garden.

The French commercial cultivator, however, found that garden beds were too small and often required greenhouses —an expensive way to farm. In the nineteenth century the French moved their beds into the caves that resulted when the stones to build Paris were quarried—hence the name champignon de Paris.

American farmers began cultivating the same species at about the same time, and continued to do so until 1926 when a farmer discovered some pure white mushrooms growing amidst his crop of buff-colored meadow mushrooms (*Agaricus campestris*). He cultivated these white mushrooms and today most of the familiar button mushrooms (*Agaricus bisporus*) we buy are their direct descendants.

Although mushrooms have been cultivated commercially in America for a little more than a century, it has been only in the last ten years or so that an interest in species other than the *Agaricus bisporus* of supermarket fame has surfaced. This has provided the incentive for commercial growers to move into the cultivation of species previously found only in the wild. Shiitakes and oyster mushrooms are now being grown commercially and soon we will find cultivated Périgord-type truffles grown in America to entice and delight our palates.

Perhaps the time is not far off when cultivated boletes, and (dare we dream it) cultivated morels will find their way to our tables. Until then, three cheers for the outdoor entrepreneurs who are making our gourmandizing so much more enjoyable.

◇   ◇   ◇

GENERAL RULES
for BUYING, PREPARING, *and* PRESERVING FRESH WILD MUSHROOMS

SHOPPING

When choosing fresh mushrooms, look for specimens that are moist but not mushy. If mushrooms are too dry (unless they have been deliberately and thoroughly dried) it usually means that they've been refrigerated for some time and have lost some of their flavor. On the other hand, mushy ones have begun to decompose and may have an unpleasant flavor, odor, and texture.

Given the cost of wild mushrooms, you should do everything you can to insure that you get good ones. Don't be afraid to smell mushrooms before you buy them. If they still have an earthy, woodsy, or mushroomy fragrance, it's a good bet that they're fresh. If their odor is neutral or nonexistent they may have lost some flavor intensity. If the odor of a mushroom is unpleasant, don't buy it. But keep sniffing; the others in the same basket may be perfectly all right.

Finally, experiment. If you see a mushroom you think you would like, don't be shy, buy it. Wild mushrooms are not likely to be carried in large quantities even by specialty stores. And he who hesitates may go mushroomless.

STORING

All wild mushrooms are best eaten as soon as possible after they're picked. Since those you find in specialty stores and supermarkets have been picked days before and kept under refrigeration, plan to use them as soon as you can. The ideal would be to buy only the amount you need and plan to cook that day, but sometimes, if the price is right or you think a particular kind won't come your way again soon, you may want to buy more than you can use immediately. Mushrooms may be stored in a paper bag (never store them in a plastic bag) in the refrigerator, but only for a few days. Put the bag on a plate and be careful not to set anything on top of it. Many fresh wilds are brittle and quite fragile, and you don't want to crush them inadvertently.

CLEANING AND PREPARATION

Everything about wild mushrooms is controversial—their names, classifications, sometimes even their descriptions—but nothing is more hotly debated in mushroom circles than the question of whether or not to wash them. Those in favor of washing argue that it in no way impairs their flavor, those against are emphatic that it eliminates certain critical flavor esters and bloats them with unnecessary water. Most professional cooks lean toward the latter position, though some concede that if the mushrooms are being used in soup, washing does not harm them. Luckily, there is a compromise solution. Probably the best way to get rid of surface dirt that clings to mushrooms is simply to wipe each cap and stem with a soft, damp cloth. Wash mushrooms under cold running water only when wiping them with a cloth is ineffective, and always dry them immediately.

To prepare fresh mushrooms for cooking, trim off the rough base of the stem with a sharp stainless steel paring knife. If the cap sits squarely on the stem as in boletes, meadow mushrooms, shiitake, and the like, separate it from the stem. Otherwise leave the mushroom whole. With a damp soft cloth (flannel is best), or a damp mushroom brush, gently brush away any dirt that adheres to the meat of both parts. (Remember that mushrooms tend to be fragile and are sometimes brittle, so be sure to handle them gently.) Slice through the cap and stem from top to bottom to check that they're not wormy or beginning to decompose, and if you see small signs of infestation or rot, cut the affected parts away. If the infestation is general, discard the mushroom. After the caps and stems have been cleaned, gently pat them dry. Your mushrooms are now ready to cook.

To prepare frozen mushrooms for cooking, remove them from their package and place them in a nonstick pan with 1 tablespoon of butter or good quality vegetable oil. Cover the pan and cook the mushrooms gently over low heat, stirring occasionally, until they are completely defrosted. Use them, and any liquor they have given off, as if they were fresh. You may have to allow a little more time to reduce their liquor than is called for in your recipe.

To reconstitute dried mushrooms, soak them in warm (not hot unless otherwise specified) water to cover for 30 minutes. Remove the mushrooms with a slotted spoon, reserving the liquid, and pat them dry. Strain the liquid through a paper coffee filter to remove sand or grit, and save (freeze it if you do not plan to use it right away) for future use as stock for sauces and soups. Reconstituted this way, most mushrooms can be used as if they were fresh.

PRESERVING

Freezing   For longer storage, clean the mushrooms as directed above, then sauté them in liberal quantities of butter (approximately 4 tablespoons of butter per cup of sliced mushrooms) for about 5 minutes over low heat. Let cool and place them in labeled freezer containers or freezer bags. Press as much air as possible out of the containers before sealing, then freeze. Frozen mushrooms will keep up to a year.

DRYING   Drying mushrooms is an easy enough process to learn. There's only one hard and fast rule to remember: Mushrooms must be thoroughly dried before you store them. If any moisture is left in them, they will eventually begin to mold and decay.

To prepare your mushrooms for drying, simply clean them as directed above or in chapters on specific varieties, cut away any portions that are not perfect, and slice them quite thin.

A window screen you're not using makes an ideal drying tray. If you don't have one, however, you can use a tray or cookie sheet lined with several layers of newspaper or paper towels. Place the mushrooms in a single layer on the paper, then set them in the sun. Turn them occasionally. If they're not completely dry in one day (and it is possible they won't be), bring them indoors before sundown. Otherwise they will absorb the moisture that develops as the air cools down and will take much longer to dry. Repeat the process until the mushroom slices are as brittle as thin tree bark. If you prefer to dry them indoors, spread the mushrooms on a cookie sheet and place them in a warm (less than 100°) oven until they resemble pieces of tree bark. Store dried mushrooms in tightly sealed plastic bags in a cool, dry place.

◇   ◇   ◇

There is nothing more beautiful than the garlands of whole dried wild mushrooms that can be found draped about the stalls in Russian or Polish markets. To make your own mushroom garland, thread whole mushrooms on heavy-duty thread such as that used for carpet mending, leaving space between each mushroom to allow the air to circulate, then hang them in a warm oven or in the sun to dry.

◇   ◇   ◇

The recipes in this book were developed to be used with specific mushrooms, but if those called for aren't available, feel free to try other species. This is not to suggest that all mushrooms taste alike. On the contrary, each has its own distinctive flavor. But they are all delicious. Using a different mushroom gives the same dish quite a different flavor accent—additional proof of their remarkable versatility.

◇   ◇   ◇

SPRING

As the days grow longer and warmer, and the snow begins to melt, foragers in the Pacific Northwest start their daily treks into the high woods and meadows looking for those edible treasures that are making our produce markets such exciting places in which to browse. At first only a few morels appear to tantalize our palates. Soon more and more arrive, until they reach their peak around the first or second week of June. Then, as their numbers begin to wane, a few beautiful, bulbous boletes appear to capture and hold our culinary attention.

What better way to celebrate the arousal of nature after winter's long sleep than with a feast of fresh spring mushrooms.

◇ ◇ ◇

MORELS

GENUS: *Morchella*
SPECIES: *esculenta, deliciosa, angusticeps, semilibera, and elata*
COMMON NAMES: Morel (Eng.); Morille (Fr.); Morchel (Ger.); Spugnola gialla (It.); Smardz jadalny (Pol.)
MARKET AVAILABILITY: Late March through May.

◇   ◇   ◇

Morels don't seem to care where they grow. They have been gathered in forests, roadsides, meadows, and under hedges in such widely assorted places as the Pacific Northwest, Maryland and Virginia, the Michigan Peninsula, and on lawns in Boston. Quite often they're found in old apple orchards and on burned ground. At the end of the nineteenth century they were reported growing "in profusion on burnt hillsides all along the Pacific coast." In Michigan they grow in such abundance that festivals are held at which the hopeful come from all over the world to hunt and eat morels. Yet, despite their seemingly ubiquitous nature, they are hard to find. Once it has been discovered, the morel's growing ground becomes a cherished secret. The story is told of an elderly Swiss spinster lady who, realizing her end was near, sent for her niece then living in America, to pass on to her the location, near Zurich, where every spring she had been gathering morels—a legacy more precious than jewels.

Morels fruit in early spring through late spring. Warm gentle rains encourage their growth, but hot, dry weather inhibits it. Unusually dry spring weather or an early heat wave will result in small crops and high prices. Unfortunately, efforts to cultivate Morels have not yet proved successful.

The Morel's honeycombed, cone-shaped cap and its cream-colored, contiguous stem make it the easiest fungus to correctly identify. Its taste makes it the most sought after fungus after the truffle.

For centuries peasant women living near the Black Forest of Germany supplemented the family income by picking them for the markets of Munich, Wurzburg, and Augsburg. Because they believed that morels grew best on burnt-over ground, the women returned to the forest each fall and started fires to insure a good crop the following spring. This placed the local authorities in a terrible quandary. They loved morels dearly but they were in danger of losing their forests. Eventually, gustatory considerations were set aside. Strict laws were passed prohibiting such fires, and the forests of Bavaria were saved from virtual extinction at the hands of overzealous housewives.

Polish folklore explains the morel's peculiar appearance with the tale of the witch who angered the devil one day. In a fury he chopped her up into little pieces and flung her to the wind. Everywhere a piece landed a wrinkled mushroom appeared that looked just like the little witch.

Because of their deep and earthy flavor, morels are often paired with cream or white wine sauces and mild-flavored meats such as veal or chicken. But they are also perfect partners with grilled and roasted foods.

When first confronting a morel the second question anyone asks is: "How do I get them clean?" (The first question: "Is it edible?" Some species that look like morels are poisonous.) Use only as much water as is necessary to get rid of the grit. Carefully and gently wipe them with a damp soft brush or cloth. Since true morels are hollow from the base of their stems to the tip of their caps, you can slice them lengthwise and clean the interior in the same manner. To wash large morels you are planning to stuff, just swish a little water around the inside and let them drain. If you find one that isn't hollow, *do not eat it.* The stem of the deadly false morel is not completely hollow nor is it contiguous with the cap. (That is, the cap sits *on top* of the stem, and is not one with it.) While people claim to be able to eat some species of false morels with no ill effects, most of us are likely to suffer severe gastrointestinal problems. False morels contain a chemical compound akin to rocket fuel, and very special handling is required to neutralize or eliminate it. It is best to avoid them.

One final word of caution. Never eat morels, or for that matter any wild mushroom, raw. You may end up with an upset stomach that cooking could have prevented.

Fresh Morel Soup

Morels produce a rich-tasting soup and this version makes excellent use of their dense, almost smoky flavor. It has the added advantage of being remarkably easy to prepare.

Serves 4

8 ounces small morels
3 tablespoons clarified butter
1 tablespoon finely chopped shallots
1 sprig fresh thyme
1 small bay leaf
1 tablespoon flour
4 cups rich chicken stock (page 192) or canned chicken broth
1 large egg yolk
1 cup crème fraîche (page 194) or sour cream
4 sprigs fresh tarragon

1.   Slice the morels in half lengthwise and wipe them thoroughly clean, inside and out, with a damp cloth or brush. Pat them dry and set aside.

2.   Melt the butter in a large saucepan for which you have a tight-fitting cover, add the shallots, and sauté them until tender. Add the morels and toss to coat them in the butter. Place the thyme and bay leaf on top of the morels, cover the pan, and sweat the mushrooms over low heat for 3 to 5 minutes. Uncover, discard the thyme and bay leaf, and sauté, stirring, 3 minutes longer. Sprinkle the mushrooms with flour and blend well.

3.   Stirring continuously, add the chicken stock to the mushrooms a little at a time, then cover the pan and simmer the mushrooms slowly for 30 minutes.

4.   In a large bowl, beat the egg yolk with a wire whisk until creamy. Then add the crème fraîche and beat until smooth. Slowly add the hot soup to the egg/cream mixture, stirring continuously with the whisk.

5.   Ladle the soup into individual bowls, float one sprig of tarragon in each bowl, and serve immediately.

VARIATION: Dried morels may be substituted for fresh in this recipe. See page 177 for the best way to reconstitute morels.

◇   ◇   ◇

Morels in Cream

(MORILLES À LA CRÈME)

The classic treatment for morels is to cook them in cream sauce. This dish is lovely as a first course served over toast, in a puff pastry shell, or on pasta, or you can use it as is done in Europe, as a sauce over grilled meat.

Serves 4

12 ounces fresh morels
 1 tablespoon water
 4 tablespoons unsalted butter
½ teaspoon salt
⅛ teaspoon freshly ground black pepper
 1 grating of fresh nutmeg or to taste
 1 tablespoon Armagnac or Cognac
 2 large egg yolks, slightly beaten
¾ cup heavy cream or very thick sour cream

1. Wipe the morels as described on page 19 and cut them lengthwise into quarters. Place them in a heavy-bottomed saucepan for which you have a cover and sprinkle with the water. Cover the pan tightly and sweat them over low heat for approximately 10 minutes. (This draws out their liquid and intensifies their flavor.) Drain the morels, reserving 1 tablespoon of the liquid. Set morels aside.
2. Using the same saucepan, melt the butter over low heat, add the morels, raise the heat to moderate, and toss until they are completely coated with the butter. Sprinkle with the salt, pepper, and nutmeg, then add the Armagnac and the reserved mushroom liquid. Reduce heat to low, cover tightly, and cook very slowly for approximately 20 minutes.

3.   Combine the egg yolks and cream in a small bowl and blend thoroughly. Add this mixture to the mushrooms and, stirring constantly, cook over low heat for about 5 minutes, or until the sauce thickens. Never allow the sauce to boil. Taste, correct seasoning, and serve.

NOTE: To make the morels even more compatible with roasts, add 1 to 2 tablespoons of the meat juices (clear of fat) to the mushrooms before adding the cream.

Paula Wolfert's Asparagus with Black Morels

Paula Wolfert is unquestionably one of America's best food writers. Her food and travel articles that appear in America's leading food and life-style magazines are always a delight. But it's as a cookbook writer that she excels. Not only is her style informative (one never fails to learn a new technique), but her recipes are always unmistakably her own. Notice, when you prepare this dish, how simple yet how "right" it is.

Serves 5 or 6

12 ounces fresh dark morels, stems removed, cut in half
    if large
 2 tablespoons unsalted butter
 1 tablespoon lemon juice
   Salt and freshly ground white pepper
 3 dozen asparagus, preferably of similar thickness
½ cup crème fraîche (page 194)
 2 teaspoons sherry or port
12 sprigs Italian parsley

1. Wash the fresh morels in acidulated water; swish to release dirt, drain, and pat dry.

2. In a 9-inch nonstick or well-seasoned skillet, cover and slowly cook fresh morels with 2 tablespoons butter, 2 tablespoons water, lemon juice, and salt and pepper for 12 to 15 minutes or until the moisture has evaporated. Shake the skillet often to avoid sticking. Set aside.

3. Wash asparagus under running water, break off the bottom portion of each stalk and peel using a paring knife or a swivel-bladed peeler. Cook asparagus until crisptender in boiling salted water (the time depends upon thickness and age of the asparagus). Drain on a kitchen cloth, cover, and keep warm.

4. Just before serving, add crème fraîche to the morels and reduce by boiling to one-half. Stir in sherry or port and adjust seasoning. Pour over the asparagus, strew with torn bits of flat leaf parsley, and serve at once.

NOTE: Combine 2 tablespoons vinegar or lemon juice with 1 quart water to make acidulated water.

VARIATION: Substitute 2 ounces dried morels; macerate trimmed dried morels in 1½ cups water for 2 hours, squeeze dry, and set aside. Strain soaking liquid through filter paper and reserve. Thoroughly rinse morels under running water to remove any sand. Combine reserved soaking liquid and morels in skillet and bring almost to a boil, simmer 5 minutes or until liquid has evaporated. Add butter, water, lemon juice, and seasoning and prepare as directed above.

◇   ◇   ◇

Morels Stuffed with Shrimp Mousse

Filling morels with forcemeat is the second most popular way of preparing them after cooking them in cream. Their hollow caps invite stuffing and nearly every culture has its own way of doing it. This recipe is my favorite, because of the taste and textural contrasts it affords.

Choose fresh morels with the largest caps you can find (usually the esculenta or deliciosa) so that you get more than just a taste of the remarkable forcemeat. Two of these very rich mushrooms are adequate as a first course; four, served with steamed vegetables, make an elegant main course.

Makes 16 mushrooms

16 very large morels
10 medium shrimps, shelled and deveined
10 medium scallops, tough muscles removed
 2 shallots
¾ cup heavy cream
¾ teaspoon kosher salt
⅛ teaspoon freshly ground black pepper
 2 tablespoons unsalted butter
 2 teaspoons finely chopped fresh dill

1.   Preheat oven to 350°.
2.   Gently wipe the morel caps and stems. Cut the stem off at the base of the cap and save for another use. Swish a little water inside each cap to remove any sand or grit and stand the caps upright on several layers of paper towels to drain.
3.   Cut the shrimps, scallops, and one of the shallots into quarters. Fit a food processor with the metal chopping

blade, and pulsing the machine on and off, chop each quarter shallot until finely minced. Add the shrimps and scallops and process 1 minute. Scrape down the sides and process 30 seconds longer. Scrape down the sides again, then continue processing while slowly adding ¼ cup of the heavy cream. Turn off the machine, scrape down the sides, add salt and pepper, and start processing again. Add more cream—but no more than ¼ cup—a little at a time, until the mixture is like stiff whipped cream. Do not allow it to liquefy.

4.   Mince the remaining shallot and combine it with the remaining cream in a small saucepan. Scald the cream (cook just until bubbles appear on the edge of the cream) and immediately remove it from the heat. Set the flavored cream aside.

5.   Fill a pastry bag fitted with a straight tube with the forcemeat, and squeeze enough into each morel to fill. Stand the morels upright in a buttered baking dish just large enough to hold them and pour the flavored cream into the dish. Melt 1 tablespoon butter and drizzle it over the morels. Cover and bake in the preheated oven for 10 minutes. Baste with the pan liquids and bake 5 minutes longer. Remove the morels and keep them warm.

6.   Transfer the cream sauce remaining in the baking dish to a small saucepan and cook until it is reduced slightly and begins to thicken. Add the remaining tablespoon of butter and stir until completely incorporated. Stir in the dill. Spoon some sauce onto each plate and serve the morels upright on the sauce.

NOTE: The forcemeat may be prepared in advance and refrigerated until ready to use. Don't wash the mushrooms until you are ready to use them because the extra moisture may cause them to decay quickly.

Morel-stuffed Artichokes

Served with fresh tomato coulis (see recipe below), a medium-sized artichoke makes a delightful first course, while the large globes constitute a magnificent vegetarian main course.

Serves 4 as a main course
6 as a first course

6 ounces fresh morels
4 large globe or 6 medium-sized artichokes
Juice of 1 lemon
1 tablespoon flour
4 tablespoons unsalted butter
1 large sourdough English muffin (2 ounces), split and lightly toasted
1/3 cup heavy cream
1/2 teaspoon kosher salt
1/8 teaspoon freshly ground black pepper
1 teaspoon chopped fresh tarragon, or 1/4 teaspoon dried
1 egg, slightly beaten

1.   Wipe the morels with a damp cloth or brush, trim, and chop them coarsely. Set aside.
2.   To prepare the artichokes for stuffing, break off the first three layers of leaves around the base, rubbing the broken areas with the lemon juice. Then slice off the tops of the remaining leaves level with the broken leaves. Trim the stem level with the base and rub all over with lemon juice. Then put the artichokes in an enameled or stainless steel saucepan just large enough to hold them. Add enough water, mixed with the flour, to cover the artichokes, then add the remaining lemon juice and bring to a boil. Lower

the heat and simmer 30 to 40 minutes or until the bottoms of the artichokes are just tender and the chokes can be pulled out easily.

3. Drain the artichokes, bottoms up, on several layers of paper towel. Remove the chokes and all but two outer layers of leaves. Set aside.

THE FILLING

1. Melt the butter in a nonstick skillet over low heat. Add the morels and sauté, stirring, 1 minute. Cover and continue cooking for 10 minutes.

2. Using your hands, break the English muffin up into coarse crumbs. Add the crumbs to the mushrooms and mix until all the liquid is absorbed.

3. Transfer the mushroom/crumb mixture to a small bowl and add the remaining ingredients. Mix thoroughly, divide into enough equal portions for the number of artichokes, and fill each artichoke.

4. Place the filled artichokes in a well-buttered baking dish, add enough water to cover the bottom of the pan, and bake in a 350° oven for 15 minutes. Place each artichoke on a bed of fresh tomato coulis.

VARIATION: ½ ounce of dried imported boletes (cèpes or porcini), reconstituted, may be substituted for the morels.

◇   ◇   ◇

TOMATO COULIS

Approximately 2 cups

3 large very ripe tomatoes (approximately 1 pound)
3 tablespoons extra virgin olive oil
1 medium onion, finely chopped
1 shallot, minced
1 clove garlic
½ tablespoon tomato paste
1 tablespoon dry white wine
⅛ teaspoon sugar
3 tablespoons chopped fresh basil, leaves only (see note)
Salt and freshly ground black pepper to taste

1.   Bring 7 cups of water to boil in a 3-quart saucepan. Drop the tomatoes in the boiling water and scald them for 15 seconds. Remove them with a slotted spoon and immediately immerse them in ice cold water to stop the cooking.
2.   Trim the stem ends and slip or peel the skins off. Slice each tomato in half horizontally and press the seeds out with your fingers. Chop the meat coarsely and set aside.
3.   Heat the oil over low heat in a 2-quart heavy bottomed saucepan. Add the onion and shallot. Squeeze the garlic into the pan with a garlic press. Add the vegetables, cover and cook until the onions are soft but not colored, about 2 or 3 minutes. Add the tomatoes and tomato paste. Stir to mix completely, cover and cook over low heat for 20 minutes.
4.   Transfer the cooked vegetables to the container of a food processor fitted with a metal blade. Purée.
5.   Return the purée to the saucepan and add the wine,

sugar, and basil and mix. Cook over low heat an additional 7 minutes to thicken slightly. Season with salt and pepper to taste and return the purée to the food processor fitted with a metal blade. Pulse the processor on and off 4 times. Return the purée to the pan and reheat it gently 2 minutes before using.

NOTE: If fresh basil leaves are not available, use fresh parsley instead. Do not use dried basil.

Veal Stew with Morels

(Stufato di Vitello e Spungole)

In Tuscany where bistecca *is king there exists a veal casserole that refuses to bend its knee to the reigning monarch. Serve this dish on a bed of very clean, quickly blanched, drained fresh spinach. It is nothing less than spectacular.*

Serves 4 to 6

    2 tablespoons unsalted butter
    3 tablespoons extra virgin olive oil
    3 shallots, coarsely chopped
  ¾ pound small morels, trimmed and cleaned
1½ pounds lean veal, cut into 1-inch cubes
    2 tablespoons all-purpose flour
    3 tablespoons good quality Italian tomato paste
    2 tablespoons veal stock (page 190) or rich chicken stock (page 192)
  ⅓ cup dry Italian white wine
    1 teaspoon salt
  ⅛ teaspoon freshly ground black pepper
    1 tablespoon brandy
  ¼ cup finely chopped parsley

1.   Heat the butter and oil in a dutch oven for which you have a cover. Add the shallots and cook 30 seconds until just softened. Add the morels, toss well to coat, cover, and cook over medium heat for 5 minutes. Using a slotted spoon, remove the morels and shallots and set aside.

2.   Dredge the veal in the flour. Reheat the oil and butter in the same dutch oven you used to cook the morels and brown the veal cubes over moderately high heat. Meanwhile, dilute the tomato paste with the stock and set aside.

3.   When the veal is browned on all sides return the shallots and morels to the pan; add the wine, and cook over moderate heat until the wine is reduced by half. Add the salt and pepper and gently stir in the tomato paste. Lower the heat, cover, and continue to cook 35 to 45 minutes or until the meat is tender. Do not overcook.

4.   Before serving, heat the brandy, ignite, and pour it over the meat. Toss, sprinkle with parsley, and serve.

VARIATION: Substitute meadow, oyster, or hedgehog mushrooms for ¼ cup of the morels.

◇ ◇ ◇

BOLETES

GENUS: *Boletus*

SPECIES: *edulis* and *mirabilis*

COMMON NAMES: Boletes, King Boletes, Polish mushroom (Eng.); Cèpe (Fr.); Steinpilz, Herrenpilz (Ger.); Porcino (It.); Borowik szlachetny (Pol.)

MARKET AVAILABILITY: In June, then again late September, October and November

◇　◇　◇

Boletes are found scattered under conifers or a mixture of hardwoods and conifers from New York and New England to the Rocky Mountains and as far west as the Pacific Coast and Alaska.

These meaty mushrooms, so prized in classical cuisine, appear in late spring through early summer and again in early fall. This second coming is particularly welcome because it is often even more abundant than the first.

When you come across their large convex rusty brown caps sitting squarely on fat clublike white stalks, you know you're in the presence of one of the most sought-after edibles in the world—the king bolete. Do not hesitate— buy them and take them home. When you plan to use them, wipe them clean with a damp cloth. If the undersides of the caps (the pores) are mushy, scrape them out with a teaspoon as you would the choke of an artichoke. Trim the tough base of the stems and pat them dry. They're now ready to be cooked. If the pores are firm, you needn't remove them.

Some years ago my husband and I were living in a Swiss mountain village best known for its air-dried meat and jet-set residents. Two of my nieces, then in their early teens, came to stay with us and we were suddenly faced with the dilemma of finding ways to amuse them.

Sensing our limited experience with teenagers, a dear friend came to the rescue. "Why don't they come mushroom hunting with Fredi and me?" Fredi, her husband, had been born and bred in the village and like most locals knew the mountains as well as his own front yard. "Perfect!" we thought, "they'll be safe and doing something they have never done in the San Fernando Valley."

The girls arose early the next morning, displaying only the barest enthusiasm. Despite their reluctance we insisted, and off they went. We were certain they'd be back tired, frustrated, and empty-handed, but better for having spent the day outdoors.

To our surprise they returned that afternoon, hair disheveled, arms and legs covered with scratches, but almost hysterical with joy. Clutched in their hands was a huge wooden basket filled with rotund cinnamon-colored mushroom caps—the most beautiful boletes we'd ever seen.

That evening, only slightly less hysterical, we all joyously sat down to devour their "catch."

Since then we've enjoyed many, many Boletes picked, however, in the comfort of our own fine food shops. While my nieces agreed it was fun hunting them, the real fun was in the eating.

◊   ◊   ◊

Boletes and Beef Consommé

Save this easy-to-prepare consommé for a time when you have accumulated a supply of the liquid left over from reconstituting dried boletes. It makes a lovely first course.

Serves 4

2 small fresh boletes or 1 medium-sized fresh bolete
¾ cup liquid in which dried boletes have been reconstituted, strained
1 can condensed beef consommé with gelatin (not beef broth)
2 tablespoons Madeira wine
4 paper-thin slices fresh lemon for garnish

1. Wipe the boletes clean with a damp cloth and trim the base of the stems. Keeping the cap and stem intact, slice the mushrooms very thinly. Combine the mushroom slices and the soaking liquid in a small saucepan. Bring the liquid to a soft rolling boil and cook for 2 minutes.
2. Meanwhile, combine the consommé, 1 can of water, and the wine in a 1-quart saucepan and bring to a boil. Lower the heat and simmer for 5 minutes.
3. Using a slotted spoon, remove the mushroom slices from the reduced soaking liquid and set them aside. Skim off any froth or scum that may have formed on the liquid. Add the mushroom liquid to the consommé, stir, and simmer 1 minute longer.
4. Ladle the consommé into individual serving bowls. Float one slice of lemon in each bowl and garnish with the cooked mushroom slices. Serve immediately.
NOTE: This consommé can be turned into a rich sauce for meat or fish as follows: Combine 2 tablespoons

butter with 1½ tablespoons flour and add this roux to 1¼ cups consommé. Bring to a boil, stirring continuously, then reduce the heat and cook just until the sauce is thick enough to coat a wooden spoon.

VARIATION: Shiitakes or meadow mushrooms may be substituted for the fresh boletes.

Grilled Porcini

The versatility of this fleshy mushroom accounts for its many uses in the kitchens of every European country. The easiest and one of the most satisfying presentations is this classic Tuscan treatment, which is as delicious in our day as it was in Leonardo's. Serve these simply grilled porcini as a first course. They are a marvelous prelude to a meal.

Serves 4

1 garlic clove, crushed
½ cup extra virgin Italian olive oil
4 very large bolete caps, 3 or 4 inches in diameter, or 12 medium caps
Kosher salt
Freshly ground black pepper
1 lemon cut into quarters

1. To flavor the oil, combine the garlic and olive oil in a screwtop jar, cover the jar, and set it aside at room temperature for at least 24 hours.
2. Using as little water as possible, gently wipe the mushroom caps with a damp cloth and pat dry with paper towels. (Save the stems for another use.) Let the caps macerate in the flavored oil for 30 minutes.

3.   Prepare a grill or hibachi with hot coals. (A handful of hickory shavings, mesquite, or other aromatic wood chips may be added to the fire for additional flavor.) When the coals turn white, brush the grill with a little oil. Place the caps, topside down, on the hot grill, and brush them with the flavored oil. Grill the mushrooms 5 minutes on one side, then turn them over and cook an additional 5 minutes or until they are cooked through. Brush tops with a little of the remaining oil and sprinkle with salt and pepper to taste. Serve with a wedge of lemon.

NOTE: Cooking time will vary depending on the size of the mushroom caps and the condition of the coals. The cooked mushrooms should be the consistency of very tender meat.

VARIATION: This treatment can be given to most large cap-on-stem mushrooms.

◇   ◇   ◇

Mushrooms Braised in Olive Oil
(FUNGHI TRIFOLATI)

I first ate porcini while living in Rome on a young professor's salary. Prices then (by today's standards certainly) seemed reasonable; nevertheless, our income precluded going to restaurants often. However, we did occasionally treat ourselves to a meal at the neighborhood tavola calda—*a small shop serving a variety of hot dishes meant to be either eaten on the premises or hurriedly taken home. My favorite dish was porcini awash in flavorful green olive oil, redolent with garlic. It seemed to epitomize the very essence of the earth of Italy. Served at room temperature, this dish makes a memorable companion to any grilled meat, poultry, or fish.*

Serves 4

- 1 pound fresh boletes
- 2 tablespoons dry white wine
- 2 cloves garlic, finely minced
- ½ cup extra virgin Italian olive oil
- 1 teaspoon anchovy paste
- Salt and freshly ground black pepper to taste
- ¼ cup Italian parsley, leaves only, washed, dried, and finely chopped

1.   Gently wipe the mushrooms with a damp cloth or brush. Trim the base of the stems and separate them from the cap. Slice the caps, then slice the stems lengthwise. Set aside.

2.   In a small nonstick saucepan, combine the wine and the garlic and cook, covered, over low heat for 1 minute. Raise the heat to moderate, add the oil, stir in the anchovy paste, and cook 1 or 2 minutes longer. Do not allow the garlic to color. Remove the pan from the heat.

3.   Arrange the mushrooms (stems on the bottom) in a small earthenware baking dish for which you have a lid. Pour the flavored oil over the mushrooms and cover the dish with a piece of buttered parchment paper cut to fit the opening of the baking dish. Place the lid on top of the paper to make a good seal. Place the dish in a preheated 350° oven and bake for 30 minutes. Remove from oven, let cool to room temperature without removing lid, then uncover and discard the paper. Season with salt and pepper to taste, sprinkle with chopped parsley, and serve.

NOTE: A wonderful composed salad can be made by arranging these warm funghi on a bed of radicchio and arugula accompanied by peppered goat cheese. Sprinkle all with chopped fresh basil and just a touch of balsamic vinegar.

VARIATION: Meadow, shiitake, or hedgehog mushrooms may be substituted for boletes.

Bolete and Goat Cheese Tart

This is light to the point of being ethereal, yet rich enough to satisfy the hungriest guest. Like Botticelli's La Primavera *it speaks of joy and renewal.*

Serves 8

CRUST
12 wheatmeal digestive biscuits, finely crushed
 5 tablespoons unsalted butter, melted

Mix the biscuit crumbs and butter thoroughly. Press them into a 10 inch quiche or tart pan, so that the crust covers the bottom and sides completely. Place the pan in the refrigerator or freezer to set.

MUSHROOM AND CHEESE FILLING

½ pound fresh boletes
3 tablespoons unsalted butter
1 tablespoon extra virgin French olive oil
½ teaspoon salt
  Pinch of cayenne
1 teaspoon freshly squeezed lemon juice
8 ounces Montrachet or a similar imported goat
  cheese, at room temperature
4 ounces cream cheese, at room temperature
3 whole eggs, at room temperature
3 tablespoons all-purpose flour
⅓ cup whole milk
¾ cup heavy cream

GARNISH

2 small leeks, trimmed and thoroughly washed
¼ small sweet red pepper

1.   Using a damp soft cloth or brush, wipe the boletes carefully. Trim the base of the stems and any parts of the caps or their underside (the pores) that appear past their prime. Remove the stems and slice them thinly, lengthwise. Slice the caps thinly. Reserve the caps and stems separately.

2.   Heat the butter and oil in a medium-sized skillet for which you have a cover. When the butter has melted, add the stems and sauté over moderate heat, stirring gently, for 3 minutes. Add the caps and toss, then sprinkle with the salt, cayenne, and lemon juice. Cover, reduce heat to low, and cook 10 minutes longer. Uncover, raise the heat to moderate, and cook until all the liquid in the pan has evaporated. (Cooking time will vary depending upon the

moisture content of the mushrooms.) Remove from heat and let cool to room temperature.

3. Cream the cheeses together in the large bowl of an electric mixer, then, one at a time, add the eggs, beating well between additions to incorporate. Sprinkle on the flour, add the milk, and continue beating until the custard is creamy.

4. Place the custard into the top of a double boiler over hot (not boiling) water. Cook, stirring continuously, until the custard is quite thick. Remove from heat and let cool completely.

5. In the small bowl of an electric mixer, whip the cream until stiff, then transfer to a larger bowl. Fold one large spoonful of whipped cream into the cooled cheese custard, then gently fold the custard into the remaining cream.

6. To assemble the tart, cover the bottom of the crumb crust with the sautéed mushrooms. Carefully spoon some filling over the mushrooms, then add the remaining filling. Smooth the top of the tart with a spatula and refrigerate at least 2 hours or until set.

7. Cut the leeks into julienne strips about 3 inches long and blanch for 30 seconds in boiling water. Remove the strips from the water, immediately plunge them into cold water, then drain and pat dry. Repeat this process with the red pepper. Garnish the top of the tart generously with the leeks and red pepper and serve.

NOTE: Green onions may be substituted for the leeks. If this is done, reduce the blanching time by half.

VARIATION: Any other wild mushroom or combination of them may be substituted for the boletes.

◇　　◇　　◇

Sauté of Snails and Boletes

(Cassolettes d' Escargot avec Cèpes)

François Dionot, director/owner of L'Académie de Cuisine in Bethesda, Maryland, is known by his students as a creative teacher and remarkable expositor of technique and innovative cooking. Among his peers in the food world he is known as a gentle and extremely generous colleague who is never too busy to be of help. In addition to his activities as teacher and administrator he is the president-elect of the International Association of Cooking Professionals. His recipe, which follows, combines clarity and creativity with uncompromising good taste.

Serves 6

3 firm, ripe tomatoes
3 dozen escargots
½ pound cepes or any other wild mushroom
2 ounces unsalted butter
4 tablespoons chopped shallots
  Salt and pepper
  Thyme
  Cayenne
1 tablespoon Armagnac
1 clove garlic, finely chopped
1 cup crème fraîche (page 194)
2 tablespoons chopped parsley

1.   Peel and seed the tomatoes and cut them into small cubes. Drain the escargots and rinse them under cold water. Clean the mushrooms and slice them thinly.
2.   Melt 1 ounce of butter in a sauté pan, add the shallots, and cook over medium heat for 2 minutes. Add the mush-

rooms and sauté for 5 minutes over high heat. Add the tomatoes and continue cooking until the tomatoes have rendered most of their juices. Season with salt, pepper, thyme, and cayenne.

3.   Add the escargots and cook them 2 minutes. Stir in the Armagnac and the garlic. Add the crème fraîche and let it boil 1 or 2 minutes more until the cream thickens a little. Swirl in the remaining butter and sprinkle with parsley. Serve in small cassolettes or on individual plates.

◇   ◇   ◇

Boletes Hidden in Chicken Mousse

(MOUSSELINE DE CÈPES CACHÉS)

Though it requires little work to prepare, this dish is sophisticated and elegant. The colors are breathtaking and the flavor and velvety texture of the fruits and chicken provide a wonderful contrast to the mushrooms. This dish was inspired by the great teacher-chef François Dionot, whose recipe you will find on page 42.

Serves 4 as a main course
      8 as a first course

   6 ounces fresh boletes
   6 tablespoons extra virgin olive oil
   2 tablespoons finely minced shallots
   2 tablespoons demiglace (see recipe below)
   2 tablespoons Madeira wine
1¼ cups heavy cream
   6 chicken thighs, skinned and boned
   2 shallots, finely minced
   1 teaspoon kosher salt
 ⅛ teaspoon freshly ground pepper
1½ tablespoons Cognac
    Butter
   1 large, very ripe mango
   1 firm, ripe avocado
    Lemon juice

1.   Wipe the boletes with a damp cloth or brush. Separate the caps and stems. Keeping them separate, chop both coarsely. Set aside.

2.   Heat the oil in a small saucepan for which you have

a cover. Add the 2 tablespoons minced shallots and cook them just until tender. Add the chopped mushroom stems and cook 1 minute, stirring, over low heat. Add the chopped caps and cook, stirring, 30 seconds longer, then cover and cook an additional 10 minutes.

3.   Stir in the demiglace and the Madeira and cook 2 or 3 minutes. Add ¼ cup of the cream and continue cooking, stirring occasionally, until the sauce begins to thicken. Correct seasoning and set the mixture aside to cool.

4.   Remove the veins and membranes from the chicken thighs. Cut the meat into cubes and combine it with the 2 minced shallots. Place the chicken in the bowl of a food processor fitted with the metal blade and process, scraping down the sides occasionally, until the chicken begins to leave the sides of the bowl. Continue processing as you slowly add the remaining 1 cup cream. The forcemeat should be very thick and moist and should hold its shape, (about the consistency of pâte à choux). Add the salt, pepper, and Cognac. Pulse the machine once or twice to mix thoroughly. Place the bowl in the refrigerator while you prepare the ramekins.

5.   Butter 8 ramekins. Fit a pastry bag with a straight tube and fill it with the chicken forcemeat. Starting in the center, pipe the forcemeat in a continuous spiral to cover the bottom and sides of the ramekin, leaving a cavity in the center to hold the mushroom sauce. Fill the cavity with the sauce and pipe additional forcemeat over it to cover. Smooth the top with a knife.

6.   Place the filled ramekins in a hot water bath (bain-marie) and bake in a preheated 350° oven 15 minutes or until the mousseline is quite firm to the touch. Remove from the water and keep warm.

7.   Peel the mango and purée the flesh. Set aside.

8.   Peel the avocado, cut it in half lengthwise, and remove the stone. Cut the halves in half again lengthwise. Rub each quarter avocado gently with lemon juice to prevent browning. Make three cuts lengthwise in each quarter avocado but do not cut through to the narrow end. Fan each piece out and sprinkle with more lemon juice.

To serve, divide the mango purée among 4 plates. Spread the purée out evenly toward the rim of the plate. Turn the ramekins out and arrange 2 mousselines on each plate. Garnish with an avocado fan. (If you serve these as a first course, divide the avocado into eighths and serve 1 mousseline per person.)

VARIATION: 1 ounce reconstituted dried boletes or morels may be substituted for fresh boletes.

DEMIGLACE
    2 tablespoons clarified butter or meat drippings
    1 tablespoon all-purpose flour
    2 tablespoons tomato paste
2½ cups rich beef stock (page 190) or good quality
        canned beef broth
        Salt and freshly ground black pepper to taste
    1 tablespoon unsalted butter

1.   Melt the butter or meat drippings in a heavy-bottomed saucepan and remove from the heat. Stir in the flour until it is completely incorporated, then return the pan to low heat and cook until the roux turns a light brown. Do not allow it to burn.
2.   Dissolve the tomato paste in the stock and, stirring continuously with a wire whisk, slowly add the stock to the roux. Raise the heat to moderate and, stirring continuously, bring the sauce just to the boiling point. Lower the

heat and simmer until the sauce is reduced to about 1 cup (approximately 30 minutes).

3.   Remove the sauce from the heat. Season to taste and stir in the remaining 1 tablespoon butter until it is completely melted. The sauce should be thick enough to coat a wooden spoon easily.

NOTE: Stored in a covered container, demiglace will keep about 2 weeks in the refrigerator.

Cèpes and Ham Hunter's Style

In this classic hunters' dish, the deep earthiness of the cèpes and smokiness of the ham speak of forests and posthunt feasts. Its complex interplay of flavors requires only the simplest setting, such as a bed of buttered fresh pasta or boiled new potatoes.

Serves 4 to 6 as a main dish

1¼ pounds small or medium boletes
   1 tablespoon unsalted butter
   3 tablespoons extra virgin olive oil, preferably French
   ½ pound Westphalian or other smoked ham, diced
   3 shallots, finely chopped
   ⅓ cup imported tomato sauce
   ¼ cup dry white wine
   3 small cloves garlic, finely chopped
      Bouquet garni made up of fresh parsley, thyme, rosemary, basil, and a small bay leaf
      Salt and freshly ground black pepper to taste
      Fresh chervil, chopped (optional)

1.   If the pores on the undersides of the mushroom caps seem soft or slippery, scoop them out. Wipe the mushrooms with a damp cloth or brush. Detach the stems and save them for another use. If the caps are large, cut them into quarters, otherwise leave them whole.

2.   Heat the butter and oil in a skillet. When the butter has melted, add the mushroom caps and sauté them lightly over low heat for 5 minutes. Remove from heat, remove mushrooms with a slotted spoon, and set aside.

3.   Transfer the remaining butter and oil to a large non-stick saucepan, then combine the ham and shallots and add them to the skillet. Cook, stirring, until the shallots are softened. Dilute the tomato sauce in the wine and stir it into the saucepan. Cook 1 minute.

4.   Turn the mushrooms and any of the liquid they have given off into the saucepan, sprinkle with the garlic, and stir gently to mix. Add the bouquet garni and salt and pepper to taste. Cook over low heat for 35 minutes. Check periodically to be certain that the mixture remains moist. Add more wine if necessary. (See note.)

5.   Remove the bouquet garni and correct the seasoning. Serve over a bed of fresh pasta or with boiled new potatoes. Garnish with the chopped chervil.

NOTE: This dish should never be allowed to get too dry. On the other hand, mushrooms vary greatly in their moisture content (this is true of every species). If the dish seems to have too much sauce at the end of the cooking time, add 1 tablespoon butter into which you have blended ¾ tablespoon flour. Add this beurre manié to the sauce and cook, stirring, until the sauce begins to thicken.

LATE SUMMER
through FALL

The greatest number of edible mushrooms makes its appearance in the fields, forests, and markets of America from late July through the warm months of fall. Summer's warm rains and fall's paling sunshine create the perfect conditions for the fruiting of mushrooms.

Boletes suddenly break through their earth and leafy cover again. Chanterelles, meadow, oyster, and hedgehog mushrooms, great clusters of crispy hen-of-the-woods fungus with their feathery black tipped fronds, and the vivid yellow and orange fungus shelves known as chicken-of-the-woods all wait, deep in the forests, to be discovered.

Fall is also the time when matsutakes, the most beloved mushrooms in Japan, sometimes grace our produce stands. The white matsutakes that grow to immense size under pines in Washington and Oregon are wonderfully flavorful, meaty, and aromatic.

For venturesome cooks this is an excellent time to experiment. The recipes that follow only begin to hint at how this season's mushrooms can be treated. Does your recipe call for duxelles? Prepare it with meadow mushrooms. Sauté chanterelles and serve them with poached Atlantic salmon. They share the season. Late summer through fall is the season of plenty—the possibilities for creating superb mushroom dishes are unlimited.

◊   ◊   ◊

CHANTERELLES *and* HORNS *-of-* PLENTY

GENUS: *Cantharellus*
SPECIES: *cibarius, cinnabarinus, subalbidus*
GENUS: *Craterellus*
SPECIES: *cantharellus, cornucopioides*
COMMON NAMES OF GENUS *CANTHARELLUS*:   Chanterelle, Cinnabar, Red Chanterelle, Golden Chanterelle, Smooth Chanterelle, White Chanterelle (Eng.); Chanterelle, Girolle, Jaunotte, Crete-de-coq, Girandola (Fr.); Pfifferling (Ger.); Gallinaccio (It.); Pieprznik jadalny (Pol.);
COMMON NAMES OF GENUS *CRATERELLUS*:   Fragrant Chanterelle, Horn-of-Plenty (Eng.); Trompette-des-morts (Fr.); Herbst-Trompete, Toten-Trompete (Ger.); Cornetto, Craterella (It.); Lejkowiec dęty (Pol.)
MARKET AVAILABILITY: From June through November; in some regions as late as December and in good years well into February

◇   ◇   ◇

Chanterelles, boletes, and morels make up a gastronomic trinity. Western cooks consider them the most flavorful of all the edible mushrooms. But while morel and bolete crops are sometimes less than generous, chanterelles, with their enticing odor of apricots and flavor hinting at champagne, grow in abundance. There is hardly a place on earth where favorable conditions exist that has not been blessed with chanterelles. They appear singly or clustered in groups so large that they blanket an entire small area. They are most often found in the short grass or mossy ground under trees that filter the sun, such as beech, oak, and the conifers. It is a peculiarity of the fungus world, however, that mushrooms of the same genus and species found in different parts of the world often taste different, and that is decidedly the case with chanterelles. Those found in the Pacific Northwest and California are more akin in flavor to those found in Europe and Scandinavia while the same varieties found growing in the eastern and southeastern United States have their own distinctive taste.

The distinctive shape of the chanterelle has been compared to an umbrella turned inside out by a gust of wind. But even this characteristic varies from species to species. Some, for example red chanterelles, have only slightly depressed caps with widely spaced gill-like ridges extending down the stem. Others such as the fragrant chanterelle have deeply depressed to funnel-shaped caps but are almost devoid of gills, and as if to add to the confusion, the cornucopia shaped horns-of-plenty have no ridges at all. The area under their caps may be wrinkled or baby-bottom smooth. The color of chanterelles ranges from pale yellow to orange to deep reddish orange. Some species are deep purple, though these are not often seen in markets, and some, like the delicious horn-of-plenty, are dark brown to black.

In the eighteenth century a half bushel of horns-of-plenty sold at Covent Garden, London's produce market, for two shillings. We know that they were eaten in England then, but how much earlier these tasty fungi were eaten is not easy to say. Ancient Greek and Roman recipes call for boleti, truffles, and suilli, but don't mention chanterelles. Yet they were classified as esculent by herbalists in the Middle Ages, so cooks of that period must have known that chanterelles were edible. If they were eaten then, how were they prepared? Were they "soused" with oriental spices or sweetened with honey and almonds? The fact is, we can't be sure how any particular mushroom was treated. The *Forme of Cury,* a fourteenth century manuscript compiled by "the chef Maister Cokes of kyng Richard the Secunde," calls only for "funges," leaving the cook free to use what he could find.

Chanterelles and Smoked Ham in Cream

The classic treatment for chanterelles, like many other mushrooms, is to cook them in cream. This variation takes advantage of their slightly acidic, sometimes peppery flavor, which, in concert with the smokiness of the ham, makes this dish truly distinctive.

Serves 8 as a first course
　　　 4 as a main course

  1 pound small chanterelles
  3 tablespoons unsalted butter
  1 tablespoon virgin olive oil, preferably French
  3 shallots
  6 ounces fat Smithfield or other smoked ham, cut into julienne strips
½ cup dry white wine
½ teaspoon kosher salt
⅛ teaspoon freshly ground black pepper or to taste
½ cup heavy cream
⅓ cup loosely packed flat parsley leaves, thoroughly washed, dried, and chopped

1. Trim the chanterelles and wipe them gently with a damp cloth or mushroom brush. If the mushrooms are large, slice them lengthwise into quarters. Dry them thoroughly and set aside.

2. Melt the butter and heat the oil in a saucepan for which you have a cover. Combine the shallots and ham and add them to the pan. Cover and cook over moderately low heat for about 10 minutes or until the shallots are wilted.

3. Add the mushrooms, wine, salt, and pepper and mix gently. Cover and cook an additional 10 minutes, stirring occasionally. Uncover, and cook an additional 10 minutes. Stir in the cream and raise the heat to moderately high. Cook 3 or 4 minutes or until the sauce is reduced by half. Stir in the parsley. Correct seasoning and serve with toast triangles or in puff pastry shells.

VARIATION: A combination of 1 pound of hedgehog mushrooms and ½ pound of fresh shiitake caps, sliced and sprinkled with ½ teaspoon freshly squeezed lemon juice, may be substituted for the chanterelles.

◇   ◇   ◇

Marinated Chanterelles and Maine Shrimp

This recipe has its roots in the culinary tradition of combining the bounty of oceans and forests. Served as directed this makes a delicious cold main dish. Halve the recipe if you wish to serve it as a first course.

Serves 4 to 6

1 pound chanterelles or horns-of-plenty
1 cup dry white wine
2 thin slices lemon
3 thin slices onion
4 peppercorns
1 small bay leaf
1 pound fresh Maine or other small shrimp, shelled and deveined
  Grated rind of 1 lemon
3 tablespoons freshly squeezed lemon juice
1 small shallot
⅓ cup extra virgin French olive oil
  Kosher salt and freshly ground black pepper to taste
½ pound pousse-pied, available in specialty food stores, or other sea vegetable (see note)

1.   Wipe the mushrooms with a soft damp cloth or brush. Trim the base of the stems and cut the mushrooms lengthwise in half. (Quarter them if they are large.) If you are using horns-of-plenty cut them into large dice.
2.   Place the mushrooms in a large nonstick saucepan, cover, and sweat them over moderate heat for 2 or 3 minutes. Uncover and cook, stirring occasionally, until the mushrooms have given up all their liquid. Raise the heat

to high and cook until the pan is completely dry. Transfer the mushrooms to a small bowl and keep warm.

3.   Make a court bouillon by combining the wine, lemon slices, onion slices, peppercorns, and bay leaf in a nonstick saucepan. Bring the mixture to a boil, then lower the heat and simmer 2 minutes. Strain, return the court bouillon to the saucepan, and bring it back to a soft boil. Add the shrimp and cook just until they turn pink. Drain and keep warm.

4.   Combine the lemon rind and juice in a medium-sized ceramic or glass bowl. Squeeze the shallot through a garlic press into the bowl and add the oil a little at a time, stirring vigorously with a wire whisk between additions. Toss the mushrooms and shrimps together and add them to the marinade. Cover the bowl tightly with plastic wrap and refrigerate overnight.

5.   Remove the mushrooms and shrimp from the refrigerator and bring them back to room temperature. Just before serving, blanch the pousse-pied in boiling water for 20 seconds, then plunge it into ice water to stop the cooking process. Pat dry and place it on 4 serving plates. Spoon the mushroom and shrimps over it, moisten with some marinade, and serve.

NOTE: If pousse-pied is not available in your area, a few pieces of dried Japanese *kombu* (large, dried, flat seaweed found in many oriental food shops) may be substituted. Soak the dried seaweed in warm water for 20 minutes to reconstitute. Drain, cut or tear into pieces, and pile them on the serving plates. If sea greens are not to your liking, substitute any green leafy vegetable that appeals.

VARIATION: Except that the visual element will be changed, any other fresh mushroom may be substituted for the chanterelles.

◇   ◇   ◇

Stewed Chanterelles in Ginger Sauce

Julie Sahni is the executive chef of the Nirvana restaurants in New York City and director of the Julie Sahni Indian Cooking School. She is the author of several highly regarded Indian cookbooks and one of the leading exponents in America of Indian cuisine.

She says that Indians prefer to pick their own mushrooms and cook them immediately. Kashmiris, especially, adore fresh mushroom preparations and save them for weddings and banquets honoring great occasions. This Northern Indian main dish from the Himalayas is a delicacy that might be served at such a banquet.

Serves 6 to 8

- 5 tablespoons vegetable oil
- 1¼ cups chopped onions
- 1½ to 2 tablespoons shredded fresh gingerroot
- 2 teaspoons finely chopped garlic
- ¼ teaspoon cayenne or 3 fresh hot green chili peppers (optional)
- ¼ teaspoon freshly ground black pepper
- 8 tiny new potatoes 1 inch in diameter, about ½ pound. Slightly larger ones may be used, if cut in half and their skins left on
- 1½ pounds chanterelles, washed, trimmed, and gently patted dry
  Kosher salt to taste

GARNISH
- 1 teaspoon roasted cumin seeds, crushed (see note)
- 1½ teaspoons lemon juice
- 3 tablespoons chopped fresh coriander

1. Heat the oil in a wok or large skillet over high heat. When the oil is hot, reduce the temperature to medium hot and add the onion. Cook for 2 minutes, stirring occasionally, until most of the moisture has evaporated. Add the ginger, garlic, cayenne or chili peppers, and black pepper and stir briskly for 1 minute. Add the potatoes and toss to coat. Fry the vegetables for 1 minute. Add the mushrooms and salt and toss to mix thoroughly. Cover and cook for 15 minutes or until the potatoes are cooked and the mushrooms are dry.

2. Uncover the pan, lower the heat, and continue frying the vegetables until they look glazed. Turn off the heat and sprinkle with cumin, lemon juice, and coriander.

3. Cover the dish to keep warm at table. Serve with rice.
NOTE: Place the cumin seeds in a very small frying pan over high heat. Toast the cumin, tossing and shaking the pan, until the seeds turn several shades darker, about 3 minutes. Remove the cumin to a waiting plate. When they are thoroughly cooled, crush them in a mortar and pestle or with a rolling pin.

One large vine-ripened tomato (about ¾ pound) added to the recipe will make it more moist and more like a stew.
VARIATION: Shiitakes may be substituted, though both the flavor and visual effect will be different.

◇　◇　◇

Chanterelles and Chicken Livers with Polenta

(Gallinaccii e Fegatini con Polenta)

While the combination of wild mushrooms and poultry livers is not new, the addition of polenta makes this recipe unique, and uniquely Italian. Followed by a salad, cheese, and fruit, this makes a wonderfully appealing meal.

Serves 4

POLENTA

 2 cups skimmed milk
½ cup finely ground cornmeal
 1 teaspoon kosher salt
   Clarified butter for frying

1. Bring the milk and salt to a boil in a large nonstick saucepan. Turn the heat down to moderately low and, stirring continuously always in the same direction, very slowly add the cornmeal. Cook, stirring constantly, until the polenta becomes quite thick and completely smooth.
2. Turn the polenta onto a wet pastry board. Using a large spatula or wet wooden spoon, spread the polenta out to a thickness of about ½ inch. Let cool completely. Cut into 2-inch by 4-inch rectangles or into diamond-shaped slices and fry in clarified butter until crisp and brown on both sides. Keep warm.

◇   ◇   ◇

CHANTERELLES AND CHICKEN LIVERS

1 pound small golden or fragrant chanterelles
2 tablespoons butter
1 shallot, minced
3 tablespoons extra virgin Italian olive oil
¼ teaspoon chopped dried sage
1 pound of chicken livers, membranes removed and
    cut into quarters
    Salt and freshly ground black pepper to taste

1.   Carefully wipe the chanterelles with a damp cloth or brush, and trim the bases of the stems. Pat dry.
2.   Melt 2 tablespoons of butter in a skillet over moderately low heat. Add the shallot and cook, stirring, until it is transparent. Add the mushrooms, raise the heat to moderate, and cook until they have given up their liquid. Continue cooking until the pan is completely dry, about 5 minutes in total. Transfer the chanterelles to a small bowl and set aside.
3.   In a second skillet heat the olive oil and stir in the sage. Add the livers and sauté, over moderately high heat, until the livers are browned all over but still pink inside. Add the mushrooms and toss. Cook about half a minute, tossing. Season with salt and pepper and serve immediately with slices of polenta.
VARIATION: Sliced oyster mushrooms may be substituted in a pinch. Or 2 ounces of dried chanterelles when reconstituted should give you approximately the amount called for.

◇   ◇   ◇

Duck Liver with Chanterelles

(FOIE GRAS DU CANARD AVEC GIROLLES)

Thanks to a new generation of innovative growers and food distributors, fresh duck liver is now available in many specialty stores throughout the country. In this exciting dish the tartness of the champagne and the firm consistency of the chanterelles play wonderfully against the velvety richness of the foie gras. Since duck livers require a very short cooking time and should be served as soon as they are cooked, it is advisable to have the mushrooms prepared and the vegetables ready on plates before you cook the liver.

Serves 4

½ pound small golden or fragrant chanterelles
8 tablespoons clarified butter
2 tablespoons Madeira wine
3 tablespoons heavy cream
  Salt and freshly ground pepper to taste
1 small head radicchio, tough core removed
1 teaspoon balsamic vinegar
6 ounces fresh mâche (see note)
½ pound fresh duck liver, cut into 8 slices

1.   Wipe the chanterelles with a damp cloth or brush, and trim the bases of the stems. Pat dry.
2.   Heat 3 tablespoons clarified butter in a skillet over low heat. Add the chanterelles and sauté 7 minutes. Stir in the wine, raise the heat to moderate, and continue cooking an additional 3 to 5 minutes or until the liquid has been reduced by half. Stir in the cream. Cook 1 minute longer. Add salt and pepper to taste. Remove the pan from the

heat and transfer the mushrooms to a small bowl. Keep them warm.

3.   Shred the radicchio. In the same skillet you used for the mushrooms, heat 1 tablespoon clarified butter. Add the radicchio and cook 1 minute or until it is just tender. Remove the skillet from the heat and sprinkle the radicchio with the vinegar.

4.   Arrange the mâche and radicchio on four individual serving plates and set aside.

5.   In a skillet large enough to hold all the duck liver slices in one layer, heat the remaining 4 tablespoons clarified butter over high heat. When the butter is very hot add the duck liver slices. After you have placed the last slice of liver in the skillet, turn over the first slice you put in. Turn the remaining slices in the order in which they were put into the skillet. They should cook no longer than 10 to 15 seconds on each side. Place one slice on each prepared plate and garnish with the chanterelles.

NOTE: If mâche is not available, use Boston lettuce.

◇   ◇   ◇

Warm Sausage Salad with Chanterelles

(Würstli Salat mit Pfifferling)

This sausage salad has its roots in the baronial game hunts of the Black Forest. While the nobles were out enjoying the chase, their chefs were back in the hunting lodge preparing to satisfy their patrons' robust appetites with products from the smokehouse and the forest.

Serves 4 as a main course
      6 as a first course

- 8 ounces small chanterelles
- 7 tablespoons virgin olive oil
- 1 tablespoon unsalted butter
- 12 kosher frankfurters
- 1 large Spanish onion, peeled, thinly sliced, and separated into rings
- 3 tablespoons balsamic vinegar
- 1 teaspoon sugar
- ½ teaspoon salt
- ⅛ teaspoon freshly ground black pepper
- 2 tablespoons vegetable oil
- 2 shallots, minced
- 2 cups red cabbage, finely shredded
- ¼ teaspoon caraway seeds

1. Trim the bases of the stems and wipe the mushrooms thoroughly with a damp cloth or mushroom brush. Chanterelles sometimes require a little more water than usual to get them completely clean. If necessary run them quickly under cold water, then gently pat them dry.

2.   Heat 1 tablespoon oil and melt the butter in a small skillet for which you have a cover. Add the chanterelles, toss to coat, and cook them, covered, for 10 minutes over low heat. Uncover, raise the heat to moderate, and cook until all the liquid has evaporated. Set aside.

3.   Cook the frankfurters in gently boiling water until the casings split easily when pierced with a fork, about 10 to 15 minutes. Drain and allow them to cool slightly.

4.   Blanch the onion slices in boiling water for 30 seconds. Drain and submerge them immediately in ice water. Drain again, pat dry, and reserve.

5.   Prepare a marinade by combining the vinegar, sugar, salt, and pepper. Whisk until the sugar and salt are dissolved, then whisk in the remaining 6 tablespoons olive oil until well blended.

6.   Slice the frankfurters into ¼-inch slices. Combine them in a bowl with the onions and mix. Add the marinade, toss, and cover with plastic wrap. Marinate at least 30 minutes at room temperature. Add the cooked chanterelles and toss.

7.   Heat the vegetable oil in a large skillet or wok. Then combine the shallots and cabbage and add to the skillet. Toss and stir-fry until the cabbage is just tender but still crunchy. With a slotted spoon transfer the cabbage to a bowl, add the caraway seeds, and season lightly to taste.

8.   Place the cabbage on a serving platter or individual platter, spoon the mushrooms and sausage on top, and serve.

NOTE: This dish may be prepared ahead of time and refrigerated, then brought back to room temperature before serving.

VARIATION: Larger chanterelles or reconstituted dried chanterelles may be used. If using larger varieties, slice them into quarters lengthwise after washing. If using dried chanterelles, add ¼ teaspoon freshly squeezed lemon juice to the soaking water.

Turkey Scallops with Chanterelles

Here is a main course that is simple to prepare and delicious beyond expectation. The paired flavors of turkey and chanterelles will delight even the most demanding palate. Serve this with steamed carrots and zucchini. They add color, texture, and a touch of the garden.

Serves 4

1 pound golden or fragrant chanterelles, or horns-of-plenty
4 thick turkey cutlets
3 tablespoons all-purpose flour
2 tablespoons extra virgin olive oil
5 tablespoons butter
1 clove each garlic and shallot, finely minced
4 ounces sour cream
⅓ cup dry sherry
8 canned chestnuts, cut in halves
½ teaspoon kosher salt
⅛ teaspoon freshly ground black pepper
Freshly grated nutmeg
2 tablespoons chopped parsley

1.   Wipe the mushrooms with a damp cloth or brush and trim the bases of the stems. Cut them lengthwise into quarters. If using horns-of-plenty, cut them into large dice. Set aside.

2. Dust the turkey cutlets with the flour, shake off the excess, and set aside.

3. In a nonstick skillet large enough to hold all the turkey cutlets in one layer heat the oil and 2 tablespoons of butter. Add the turkey cutlets and brown them over moderate heat on both sides. Remove them from the skillet and keep warm.

4. Melt the remaining 3 tablespoons butter in the skillet, add the garlic and shallot, and cook about 4 minutes over low heat. Do not allow them to brown.

5. Combine the mushrooms, sour cream, sherry, chestnuts, salt, pepper, and nutmeg, and stir gently to mix. Return the turkey to the skillet, pour on the mushroom/cream sauce, cover, and cook over low heat about 30 minutes or until the turkey is tender. Sprinkle with parsley and serve immediately.

◇　◇　◇

MEADOW MUSHROOMS

GENUS: *Agaricus*

SPECIES: *campestris*

COMMON NAMES: Meadow mushroom, Pink bottom (Eng.); Champignon (Fr.); Wiesenegerling, Feldegerling, Erdgurtel Angerling (Ger.); Prataioli (It.); Pieczarka polna (Pol.)

MARKET AVAILABILITY: May through June and again from September through November; imported from Italy they are sometimes available through December

◇   ◇   ◇

This grandaddy of the first cultivated button mushrooms grows on well-fertilized lawns, in meadows and grassy verges. Meadow mushrooms make their first appearance in the spring, then again in the fall and other periods when the weather is cool and damp.

The meadow's cinnamon brown cap sits on a sturdy stem and is easily recognizable in shops. Its gills are pink when young but become milk chocolate brown as it gets older. It looks like a large, brown, open version of the white button mushrooms we find in supermarkets, but its flavor is more pungent and its meat is thicker and firmer.

Even the mycophobic nineteenth century English ate meadows. Mrs. T.J. Hussey, a Victorian naturalist, described them as "tender, succulent, friable and digestible . . . nourished on pure earth, in air redolent of wild thyme and the breath of kine, by dew which might be Fairies' nectar it is so free from the impurities of city miasma. . . ." On the other hand, Mrs. Hussey found their cultivated offspring "tough and indigestible . . . the flavour . . . as inferior as the materials given to produce it—musty straw in a cellar, or what other nook in the shape of pit or box or out of the way dungeon, can be afforded to the gipsey child of the sunny woodland pasture."

Handle meadow mushrooms with care, as their flaps (the edges of their caps) tend to be fragile. Never peel them; much of their flavor is in the upper layers of the cap. To prepare meadows for cooking, wipe them with a damp cloth, trim the bases of the stems, then carefully separate the stem from the cap. As is true of all mushrooms, the stems are more fibrous and therefore tougher than the caps. Chop the stems and slice the caps unless otherwise directed.

Meadow mushrooms have a deep, woodsy flavor, and can be used in any recipe calling for the ordinary cultivated variety. You'll be amazed at the depth of flavor they impart. They are often used in combination with other, more distinctively flavored mushrooms.

Crimini and Portobello mushrooms may be used in recipes calling for meadow mushrooms. Although both these varieties are cultivated, they have excellent flavor.

◇　◇　◇

Wild Mushroom and Vegetable Soup

This Swiss mountain soup falls into the category of "haus-gemacht" (homemade) despite the use of canned tomatoes. For busy urban folk its ease of preparation is justification enough for making it, but add to that its wonderful melange of flavors and you've got a dish you will be serving often.

Serves 4

½ pound meadow mushrooms
¼ pound chanterelles or horns-of-plenty
 3 tablespoons extra virgin olive oil
½ cup diced onions
 1 clove garlic, mashed
½ cup peeled, diced, red potatoes
¼ pound green beans, trimmed and cut into 1-inch
    pieces
 1 cup canned stewed tomatoes, with their juice
 3 large fresh basil leaves, chopped, or ¼ teaspoon
    dried
 3 sprigs fresh thyme, or ¼ teaspoon dried
 1 fresh sage leaf, or ⅛ teaspoon dried
½ bay leaf
 3 cups chicken broth
 1 egg yolk
½ cup grated Gruyère cheese
    Salt
    Freshly ground black pepper

1.   Wipe the mushrooms with a damp cloth or brush. If the chanterelles are difficult to get clean, run them quickly under cold water and pat dry immediately. Trim the bases

of the stems. Slice the meadows thinly. If the chanterelles are small, leave them whole. Cut large chanterelles lengthwise into quarters. Set the mushrooms aside.

2.   Heat 2 tablespoons of the oil in a 3-quart saucepan and add the onions, garlic, potatoes, and green beans. Sauté over moderate heat, stirring, until the onion is transparent and has begun to color, about 2 minutes. Add the remaining tablespoon of oil and the mushrooms, toss, then cover the pan and cook an additional 2 minutes over low heat. Stir the tomatoes and herbs into the chicken broth and add to the saucepan.

3.   Raise the heat to high and bring the soup quickly to a boil, then lower the heat and simmer the soup 25 minutes.

4.   Just before you are ready to serve the soup, beat the egg yolk well. Very slowly add ½ cup of the hot soup to the beaten yolk, stirring continuously. Blend well. Add the heated egg yolk/soup mixture to the soup in the pan, stirring to mix well. Correct seasoning and ladle into individual soup bowls. Sprinkle with the grated cheese and serve immediately.

VARIATION: Almost any of the cap-on-stem mushrooms may be used in combination. Oyster mushrooms would also do, but neither chicken- nor hens-of-the-woods are recommended because they might impart a bitterness to the soup.

◇   ◇   ◇

Crab Bisque with Meadows and Shiitakes

My high school cafeteria served one item daily. Regardless of what else was on the menu there was always something "we" called "mystery lump soup" and "they" called "cream of mushroom." I swore that if I survived into adulthood I would never eat mushroom soup again. Well, like many a childhood pledge which, thankfully, experience has amended, I eat mushroom soup as often as possible. To all those who have shared my childhood experience I dedicate this lovely bisque. I think you will agree it is mushroom soup with a difference.

Serves 4

1½ pounds meadow mushrooms
   ¼ pound fresh shiitakes
    4 tablespoons unsalted butter
    4 small shallots, finely minced
    3 cups half-and-half cream
    1 large bay leaf
    5 sprigs parsley
    1 whole clove
    1 tablespoon sunflower seed oil
    1 teaspoon sesame seed oil
    1 tablespoon soy sauce
    1 teaspoon sugar
      Pinch of salt
    1 tablespoon mirin (see note)
   ¼ cup warm water
    8 ounces cooked crabmeat, carefully picked over
    1 tablespoon flour
2½ cups chicken broth
    2 teaspoons chopped dill

1. Wipe the meadow mushrooms with a damp cloth. Trim the bases of the stems and chop both caps and stems coarsely. Set aside.

2. Wipe the shiitakes with a damp cloth. Remove the stems and discard. Slice the caps into 1/8-inch slices and set aside.

3. Melt the butter in a heavy nonstick 2-quart saucepan. Add the shallots and sauté just until tender. Add the chopped meadow mushrooms and sauté over moderate heat, stirring occasionally, until all their liquid has evaporated, about 10 to 12 minutes. Set aside in the saucepan.

4. Meanwhile combine the half-and-half, bay leaf, parsley, and clove in a small saucepan. Over a moderately low flame, heat until bubbles just begin to appear around the edges of the pan. Strain and set aside.

5. Combine the shiitakes, sunflower oil, sesame oil, soy sauce, sugar, salt, mirin, and water in a small saucepan. Bring to a boil, lower the heat, and simmer 15 minutes. Remove the saucepan from the heat and set aside.

6. To make the bisque, add the crabmeat to the meadow mushrooms and sprinkle with the flour. Stir to blend completely. Add the flavored half-and-half, stirring continuously until well blended. Stir in the chicken broth, correct the seasoning, and simmer over low heat for 20 minutes, stirring occasionally.

7. Strain the crabmeat bisque. Transfer the meadow mushrooms and crab, along with 1/2 cup of the bisque, to a blender or food processor fitted with a metal blade. Purée. Return the purée to the bisque and reheat slowly. Correct seasoning.

8. Reheat the shiitakes briefly, and drain. Ladle the bisque into individual bowls, garnish with the warm shiitake slices, and sprinkle with the dill. Serve immediately.

NOTE: Mirin, a sweet Japanese rice wine, may be purchased in most food shops selling oriental products.

Meadow Piroshki

The traditional piroshki is made with a heavy yeast dough that often overwhelms the flavors of the filling. This version is made with a buttery sour cream dough that flakes and melts on the tongue—a perfect container for its delicious mushroom and potato filling. Served with kapusta borscht, these piroshki elevate that lowly cabbage soup to a meal fit for a czar.

Serves 4 to 6

DOUGH
 1 cup sifted all-purpose flour
½ teaspoon salt
 4 ounces unsalted butter, cut into 8 pieces
 3 tablespoons sour cream

Combine the flour and salt and sift them into a bowl. Add all the butter and work it thoroughly into the flour with your hands. Add the sour cream and stir the dough with a wooden spoon until it forms a ball. Wrap the dough in wax paper and chill it overnight.

◇   ◇   ◇

FILLING

- 8 ounces meadow mushrooms
- 6 tablespoons rendered chicken fat, goose fat, or clarified butter
- ½ cup finely chopped onions
- ¾ cup cooked and mashed potatoes
- 1 egg yolk
- 1¼ teaspoons kosher salt
  Freshly ground black pepper to taste
- 1 egg, separated

1.   Wipe the mushrooms with a damp cloth or brush. Trim the bases of the stems, then separate the stems from the caps. Chop the stems finely, then chop the caps and set them aside separately.

2.   Heat the fat in a nonstick skillet, then add the onions and sauté over moderate heat until they begin to color. Stir in the chopped mushroom stems and cook, stirring, 2 minutes. Add the chopped caps and cook until all their liquid has evaporated. Add the potatoes and stir to mix well. Remove the pan from the heat and stir in the egg yolk and salt, mixing thoroughly. Season the filling with pepper to taste. Set aside.

TO ASSEMBLE AND BAKE

1.   Preheat the oven to 425°.

2.   Divide the dough into halves. Wrap one half in wax paper and return it to the refrigerator. On a lightly floured board, roll out the other half as thinly as possible. (With care the dough can be rolled as thin as wonton squares.) Using a 3½-inch cookie cutter or suitable substitute (see note), cut the dough into rounds, stack, and keep cool.

3.   Scrape any unused dough off the board and combine

it with the remaining half of the dough. Lightly flour the board and roll out the dough as before. Cut into rounds and stack.

4.   Place 2 teaspoons of filling in the center of each round. Brush the inside edge of the dough with the egg white, then fold the dough in half to form a crescent. Press the edges of the crescent together with the tines of a fork, then brush the top lightly with beaten egg yolk. (The piroshki may be frozen at this point. When ready to use, bake directly from the freezer until golden brown.) Place on an ungreased cookie sheet or in a shallow-rimmed baking pan and bake for 12 minutes or until golden brown. Serve hot or at room temperature.

NOTE: An empty tunafish can makes a fine pastry cutter. Simply remove the bottom of the can and wash thoroughly.

For hot hors d'oeuvres use a small 2-inch cookie cutter and 1 scant teaspoon filling.

VARIATION: Oyster mushrooms may be substituted for the meadow mushrooms.

◇   ◇   ◇

Calzone Est, Est, Est

On warm spring evenings the buildings on the Via Genova in Rome reverberate with laughter and happy conversation. On the left side of this narrow cul-de-sac is the Pizzeria Est, Est, Est, with its butcher-paper-covered tables crowded so tightly together that only sorcery explains the waiters' mobility. Directly across from the pizzeria is the Ristorante Est, Est, Est. Its starched linen tablecloths and napkins, crystal wine glasses, and silver plate await the arrival of an elegant clientele.

In summer the doors to both halves of the same establishment stand open. Tables spill out onto the sidewalk and the warm night air is heavy with the aroma of yeasty dough baking. On the right, impeccable classical Italian cuisine; on the left calzones —crisp, yeasty turnovers filled with the earthy flavors of wild mushrooms and cheese, and on each table, a chilled carafe of young white wine from the Est, Est, Est vineyards. There may be more elegant ways to dine, but few are more enjoyable.

This recipe will produce the calzones. The wine and atmosphere are up to you.

Serves 4

DOUGH
1½ cups warm water
   1 package yeast
   4 cups sifted, unbleached all-purpose flour
   1 teaspoon salt
   4 tablespoons green extra virgin olive oil

1.   Combine ½ cup of the warm (not hot) water and the yeast in a small ceramic or glass bowl and stir until the yeast is dissolved. Add ½ cup of the sifted flour and blend thoroughly. Set aside in a warm place for 30 minutes. The mixture should produce bubbles.

2. In a large glass or ceramic bowl combine the salt, 3 tablespoons olive oil, ¾ cup of the warm water, and the yeast mixture. Stir in the remaining flour and the remaining water to make a smooth but sticky dough.

3. Turn the dough out onto a lightly floured pastry board and knead for about 10 minutes, adding as little flour as possible. The less additional flour used, the lighter the dough will be. Form the dough into a ball and cover it with a dish towel.

4. Coat the inside of a large clean ceramic bowl with ½ tablespoon of olive oil. Turn the dough into the bowl and brush the surface of the dough with the remaining oil. Cover the bowl loosely with the dish towel and leave it in a warm place (an oven at no more than 100°F will do). Let the dough rise for 2 hours or until it is doubled in bulk.

5. Turn the risen dough out onto a lightly flavored board and punch it down. Knead it lightly for a few minutes until it is smooth again and divide it into 4 parts. Shape each part into a ball, and roll into 8-inch rounds ⅛ inch thick. Fill with the mushroom mixture as directed below.

FILLING
 1 pound meadow mushrooms
½ pound boletes
 4 ounces thick-sliced bacon, diced
 1 tablespoon green extra virgin olive oil
 1 teaspoon fresh thyme or ¼ teaspoon dried
   Freshly ground black pepper
 8 ounces mozzarella cheese (preferably fresh), grated
 4 ounces provolone cheese, grated
 4 ounces prosciutto, sliced paper-thin

1. Preheat oven to 500°.
2. Wipe the mushrooms with a damp cloth or brush.

Trim the bases of the stems, and separate the stems from the caps. Slice the caps thinly, then chop the stems. Set the caps and the stems aside separately.

3. Sauté the bacon in a heavy skillet until it begins to brown. Add the oil and the chopped mushroom stems, and cook over moderate heat 3 minutes, stirring. Add the sliced caps, toss, and continue to cook until they have given off all their liquid. Sprinkle with the thyme and several grindings of pepper, then raise the heat and continue to cook until all the liquid in the pan has evaporated. Remove from heat and set aside.

4. Cut the prosciutto into 2-inch strips and divide into 4 equal portions.

5. Place 1 ounce of the mozzarella on the bottom half of a pastry round, leaving about a 1-inch edge. Cover the mozzarella with ½ ounce of the provolone, then top with one portion of the prosciutto. Carefully spread ¼ of the mushrooms on the prosciutto, cover with ½ ounce of provolone and the remaining mozzarella. Carefully fold the top half of the pastry over the filling and turn the edges under ½ inch. Press the edge down with the tines of a fork to seal. Repeat with remaining 3 pastry rounds.

6. Using a large spatula, carefully transfer the calzones to a pizza pan or baking stone. (A lightly floured cookie sheet may also be used.)

7. Place the calzones in the oven and immediately lower the heat to 450°. Bake 20 minutes or until the crust is crisp and brown.

NOTE: To enhance the appearance of the calzones, some cooks brush the crusts with olive oil after removing them from the oven, but the authentic version eschews *la bella figura,* preferring to be judged entirely on taste.

VARIATION: Any combination of mushrooms may be used instead of meadow mushrooms and boletes.

Wild Mushrooms
and Eggs Gennargentu

*Sardinia's barren and forbidding interior seems an unlikely source
of exciting cuisine, yet it abounds in game and wild foods of all
kinds. Its shepherds, who often spend months away from home, de-
pend on foraging to supplement the bread and cheese they carry
with them and, as a result, a hunter's cuisine has developed. Suck-
ling pigs, birds, and mushrooms are roasted on spits over aromatic
wood fires or pan-grilled and seasoned with wild thyme and onions.*

*This rustic dish is reminiscent of Sardinian shepherds' fare and
is perfect for a Sunday brunch with friends. I prepare it in a
well-seasoned cast-iron skillet that I bring right to the table.*

Serves 4

¼ pound meadow mushrooms
¼ pound boletes
4 strips sugar-cured bacon
2 tablespoons green extra virgin olive oil
2 tablespoons unsalted butter
2 tablespoons chopped shallots
4 medium or 2 large artichoke hearts, cooked and
   trimmed (page 27), or use canned artichoke hearts
3 tablespoons imported tomato paste
¾ cup dry white wine
   Pinch freshly grated nutmeg
   Salt and freshly ground black pepper to taste
4 extra large eggs
1 ounce grated pecorino cheese
   Chili powder
2 tablespoons chopped fresh chives

1.   Wipe the mushrooms with a damp cloth or brush, trim
the bases of the stems, and slice. Set aside.

2.   Broil the bacon until crisp. Crumble and set aside.

3.   Heat the oil and butter in a medium-sized cast-iron or other skillet for which you have a cover. When the butter has melted, add the shallots and sauté them over moderate heat until they begin to color. Add the mushrooms, toss, and cook until all their liquid has evaporated.

4.   Cut the cooked artichoke hearts into small cubes and add to the skillet. Stir in the tomato paste, then add the wine, nutmeg, salt, and pepper to taste and blend thoroughly. Lower the heat, cover, and cook 5 minutes.

5.   With the back of a large spoon or ladle, make 4 depressions in the vegetable mixture. Carefully break an egg into each well. Sprinkle each egg with ¼ of the crumbled bacon and grated cheese. Place under the broiler until the cheese begins to brown. Garnish with a sprinkling of chili powder and chives and serve with hot crusty bread and butter.

Wild Mushroom and Pheasant Casserole

I can't think of pheasants without remembering a charming Swiss friend whose English occasionally let her down. She once told me with great pride that her father's favorite sport was "hunting peasants." Noting my obvious horror she continued, "Peasants, you know peasants, the ones with feathers."

Well, it's no longer necessary to hunt these tasty critters. Pheasants are farmed, and while they will probably never be as plentiful as chicken, they are available fresh in fine food stores and in the frozen food section of many supermarkets. The domesticated variety are less gamy than those caught in the wild, but they are a little meatier. You may miss the intense flavor, but the meadow mushrooms and chanterelles will provide the natural and wild element necessary in this classic hunters' casserole. Serve this with fresh cranberry or lingonberry sauce on the side.

Serves 2

12 large meadow mushrooms
24 small chanterelles, golden, fragrant, or red cinnabar
 3 tablespoons unsalted butter
 2 tablespoons extra virgin olive oil
½ cup finely chopped carrots
½ cup finely chopped onions
 1 pheasant, cut into serving pieces
 3 teaspoons all-purpose flour
 2 inner stalks of celery, with leaves, coarsely chopped
 2 cloves garlic, crushed
 1 bay leaf
 1 teaspoon fresh thyme or ¼ teaspoon dried
 1 teaspoon kosher salt
¼ teaspoon freshly ground black pepper
¼ cup calvados or pear brandy
1½ cups good red wine, such as a Bordeaux
 3 tablespoons chicken stock (page 192)
 4 ounces thick-sliced bacon, coarsely chopped
¼ cup freshly shelled walnuts, coarsely chopped
12 small white boiling onions, trimmed and peeled

1. Wipe the mushrooms with a damp cloth or brush. Trim the bases of the stems. Cut the meadow mushrooms into thick slices from the cap through the stem, combine them with the chanterelles, and set aside.

2. Heat 2 tablespoons of the butter and the oil in a nonstick skillet large enough to hold all the pheasant pieces in one layer. When the butter has melted, add the carrots and onions and cook over moderate heat, stirring, for 2 minutes. Raise heat to moderately high, add the pheasant pieces, and sauté until they are brown on all sides. Sprinkle the flour into the pan and stir to mix

thoroughly. Add the celery, garlic, bay leaf, thyme, salt, and pepper, and stir to mix.

3. Heat the calvados or brandy in a very small saucepan or in a large metal soup ladle, then pour over the pheasant in the skillet. Ignite the liquor, shake the pan, and when the flames have subsided, stir in the wine and stock, bring to a boil, then lower the heat and simmer for 30 minutes.

4. Meanwhile, melt the remaining 1 tablespoon butter in a small skillet and add the bacon and walnuts. Cook over moderate heat, stirring, until the bacon begins to brown. Transfer to small bowl and set aside.

5. When the pheasant has finished simmering, transfer it to an overproof casserole, using a slotted spoon, and add the mushrooms, bacon/walnut mixture, and boiling onions.

6. Taste the sauce in the skillet and correct the seasoning. Strain it over the pheasant, cover the casserole, and place it in a water bath (bain-marie) in a 350° oven for 20 minutes or until the meat is completely tender.

NOTE: If you use a frozen pheasant, defrost it thoroughly in the refrigerator before embarking on this recipe.

VARIATION: Three-quarters of a pound of oyster mushrooms or hens-of-the-wood fungus may be substituted for the meadows and the chanterelles.

◇　　◇　　◇

OYSTER MUSHROOMS

GENUS: *Pleurotus*

SPECIES: *ostreatus*

COMMON NAMES: Oyster mushroom (Eng.); Pleurotte
(Fr.); Austern-Seitling (Ger.); Gelone (It.); Boczniak
Ostrygowaty (Pol.)

MARKET AVAILABILITY: Both wild and cultivated varieties
are available throughout the year

◇   ◇   ◇

Oyster mushrooms, or "the shellfish of the woods," as the
English sometimes call them, can be found almost everywhere in the world, most commonly on aspen, beech, willow, and pine trees; on tree stumps, or on fallen logs; and
even occasionally on telephone poles. Under favorable
conditions they grow almost all year round—except during
the height of summer when it's too dry for them. Commercially cultivated oyster mushrooms are available in supermarkets even in summer.

Oysters are a gregarious lot. They often grow in large
overlapping rows like tiles on a roof. Their convex caps,
which can be white, buff, or silvery gray in color, sup-
posedly resemble an oyster shell, from which they get their
name. To me, they seem more like fans—with their wide,
white gills extending down to an almost nonexistent stalk.
(What passes for a stem in the mature fungus is usually
nothing more than a stubby base that is sometimes covered
with downy fur.)

The oyster's meat is thick and fleshy and mild in flavor.

Choose only moist, firm caps with a slightly mushroomy odor or no odor at all. Very fresh specimens sometimes give off a lovely odor of anise, but if the ones you buy do not have this distinctive fragrance don't be too disappointed; the fragrance of wild mushrooms begins to dissipate just a few hours after picking. Never buy oysters that feel slimy or mushy, or that have an unpleasant odor.

Like the chanterelle, this fungus was described and classified as esculent by early herbalists. But whereas chanterelles seem not to be eaten in the Far East, Oyster mushrooms are greatly favored in Japan and China and have been cultivated there for a long time.

From your first taste of this mild but flavorful fungus, you will want to use it frequently. It can be substituted in any recipe that calls for the supermarket variety.

◊   ◊   ◊

Grilled Oyster Mushrooms

Grilled foods are enjoying a deserved renaissance in the esteem of contemporary gastronomes. One of many pleasing results of this renewed interest is the variety of foods that are now feeling the heat—eggplants, peppers, squash, and, of course, mushrooms.

If you don't feel like firing up the old hibachi, these mushrooms can be pan-grilled in a well-seasoned cast-iron skillet with raised ridges with almost equally delicious results. They make a lovely first course.

Serves 6 as a first course

 1 pound large oyster mushrooms, caps only; use those
   with firm, unbroken edges
 4 to 5 tablespoons walnut oil
 1/4 cup extra virgin French olive oil
   Sea salt
   Lemon juice (optional)
   Freshly ground black pepper to taste

1. Wipe the mushrooms clean with a damp cloth or brush.
2. Make a fire in a hibachi or other such device and wait until the coals have turned white. (You may add hickory or mesquite chips or any other aromatic wood.) If you are using a cast-iron skillet, brush a little of the walnut or hazelnut oil on the pan and heat until just smoking.
3. Place the walnut oil in a small bowl. One at a time, dip each mushroom in the oil; shake lightly to remove excess oil and place the mushroom on the hot grill. Grill the mushrooms about 3 minutes on each side.
4. To serve, drizzle the caps with olive oil and sprinkle them with sea salt, or lemon juice if you prefer. Pass the pepper mill separately.

VARIATION: Any large mushroom cap can be treated this way.

Marinated Oyster Mushrooms with Smoked Salmon

Culinary historians have uncovered written evidence that marinating mushrooms is a tried and true way of preparing them. In The Closet of the Eminently Learned Sir Kenelme Digbie, Kt., *published in 1669, we find a recipe for "Pickled Champignons." This dish follows in this age-old tradition.*

Serves 8

½ pound oyster mushrooms
3 tablespoons extra virgin olive oil
3 cloves garlic, crushed
6 green peppercorns
2 whole cloves
1 sprig fresh tarragon or a generous pinch dried
1 small bay leaf
¾ cup semidry white wine
  Freshly squeezed juice of 1 lemon
1 teaspoon sugar
½ teaspoon kosher salt
⅛ teaspoon freshly ground black pepper
8 ounces of Scotch or Irish smoked salmon cut into
  paper-thin slices
4 tablespoons finely chopped Bermuda onion
1 tablespoon freshly grated or prepared *wasabi*,
  available in oriental food markets (optional)
  Radish sprouts for garnish (optional)
1 lemon cut into 8 wedges
  Freshly grated black pepper

1.   Wipe the mushrooms with a damp cloth or brush and trim the bases. Holding a sharp knife at a 45° angle, slice the mushrooms moderately thin. (This will enable you to fan out the slices when presenting the dish.)

2.   Heat the oil in a nonstick saucepan, add the garlic, and cook it over moderate heat until soft. Add the mushrooms and toss gently. Add the peppercorns, cloves, tarragon, and bay leaf. Cook, stirring, for 3 to 4 minutes.

3.   Combine the wine, lemon juice, sugar, salt, and pepper. Stir until the sugar and salt are dissolved. Stir the seasoned wine into the skillet, cover, and simmer for 10 minutes.

4.   Transfer the mushrooms and wine to a bowl, allow to cool slightly, and correct seasoning. Refrigerate at least 4 hours or overnight.

5.   To serve, place the salmon slices on individual serving plates. Arrange the thoroughly drained mushroom in overlapping slices. Garnish the plates with a mound of Bermuda onion, *wasabi* (the root of a Japanese plant, with a taste similar to horseradish), and/or radish sprouts. Pass the lemon wedges and pepper mill separately.

VARIATION: Shiitakes may be substituted for half the oyster mushrooms. This will add a somewhat chewy texture to the dish.

◇   ◇   ◇

Oyster Mushrooms and Glazed Onions

One of the best ways of serving any wild mushroom is as a vegetable course. This dish makes especially good eating with roast lamb or poultry.

  1 pound oyster mushrooms
  4 large fresh basil leaves, bruised, or 1 teaspoon dried
  1 dozen small white boiling onions, trimmed and peeled
  5 tablespoons butter
  1 teaspoon sugar
 ⅓ cup chopped yellow onion
1½ cloves garlic
  3 tablespoons sherry vinegar
  1 sun-dried tomato, drained and finely chopped
  4 large, very ripe tomatoes, peeled, seeded, and coarsely chopped
  3 sprigsfreshthyme(leavesonly),or¼teaspoondried
   Koshersaltandfreshlygroundblackpeppertotaste
   Choppedparsleyforflavorandgarnish

1. Wipe the mushrooms clean with a damp cloth or brush and trim the bases. Cut them into slices ½ inch thick and set aside.
2. Crush the fresh basil leaves in your hand and set aside.
3. Combine the white onions, 1 tablespoon of the butter, and the sugar in a small, heavy-bottomed saucepan for which you have a cover. Cover and cook over high heat for 20 minutes, shaking the pan vigorously from time to time. (The onions should be slightly caramelized, but do not allow them to burn.) Uncover and set them aside.
4. Melt the remaining 4 tablespoons butter in a large

skillet over moderately high heat until it bubbles. Add the sliced mushrooms and sauté them until they begin to color. Lower the heat and cook an additional 5 minutes. Using a slotted spoon, transfer the mushrooms to a bowl and set aside.

5.   Add the chopped yellow onions to the skillet. Squeeze the garlic through a press and add it to the chopped onions. Raise the heat to moderate and cook, stirring occasionally, until the onions begin to color. Stir in the vinegar, raise the heat to high, and cook until the vinegar evaporates, then mix in both kinds of tomatoes, basil, and thyme. Lower the heat, and cook until the vegetables have been reduced to a soft pulp, about 12 minutes.

6.   Remove the basil leaves and discard. Return the mushrooms to the skillet and add the glazed onions. Season with salt and pepper to taste and simmer an additional 2 or 3 minutes to reheat. Garnish with chopped parsley and serve.

VARIATION: Meadow mushrooms or shiitakes may be used instead of oyster mushrooms.

Spinach and Mushroom Roll

Served with a salad of radicchio and endive, this mushroom roll makes a colorful, satisfying, and relatively low-calorie meal.

Serves 4 to 6

    7 ounces oyster mushrooms
    1/2 ounce dried boletes, soaked in 3/4 cup warm water
       for 30 minutes
    1 pound fresh spinach leaves, tough stems trimmed
    4 large eggs, separated
       Generous pinch freshly grated nutmeg

½ teaspoon kosher salt
⅛ teaspoon freshly ground black pepper
2 tablespoons extra virgin olive oil
¼ cup chopped shallots
1 tablespoon all-purpose flour
½ cup whole milk
2 tablespoons freshly grated Parmesan cheese
  Butter and flour for preparing the jelly roll pan

1.   Preheat the oven to 400°.
2.   Wipe the oyster mushrooms clean with a damp cloth or brush, trim the bases, and chop coarsely. Set aside.
3.   Remove the reconstituted boleti from the soaking liquid and chop fine. Set aside. Strain the soaking liquid through a coffee filter, reserving ¼ cup. (Freeze the remaining liquid for future use.)
4.   Wash the spinach in several changes of water, if necessary, and place it in a 3-quart saucepan with only the water that clings to the leaves. Cover the pan tightly and cook over moderate heat until wilted, about 5 minutes. Drain the spinach, let cool slightly, then squeeze to remove all the liquid. Chop the spinach very fine and turn it into a mixing bowl. Add the egg yolks, sprinkle with nutmeg, salt, and pepper and mix well.
5.   Whip the egg whites until stiff but not dry, and gently fold them into the spinach.
6.   Grease a jelly roll pan with butter and place a sheet of wax paper on top, leaving a 2-inch overlap on both ends of the pan. Butter the paper and sprinkle with flour to coat, shaking off the excess. Turn the spinach mixture into the prepared pan, spreading it evenly with a spatula. Bake on the middle shelf of the preheated oven for 10 to 15 minutes, or until it is springy to the touch.
7.   While the spinach is baking, heat the oil in a medium-

sized skillet over moderate heat, add the shallots, and cook until they are soft. Add the chopped mushrooms and cook, stirring, 3 to 4 minutes. Sprinkle the flour over the mushrooms and mix well. Stirring continuously, add the milk and reserved mushroom liquid a little at a time. Lower the heat and cook 2 to 3 minutes longer or until the sauce has thickened. Season with salt and freshly ground black pepper to taste. Remove from the stove and keep warm.

8.   When the spinach roll is baked, sprinkle the surface with the Parmesan cheese, then cover the roll with a clean dish towel. Place another jelly roll pan or cookie sheet over the towel and quickly invert the pans so the wax paper is on top. Remove the top pan and gently peel off the wax paper.

9.   Reheat the mushrooms and spread them over the exposed surface of the spinach roll, leaving a 1-inch border all around. Lifting the narrow edge of the towel, gently roll the short end of the spinach away from you, as if you were making a jelly roll. Have a serving platter ready and gently roll the spinach mushroom roll onto it. Serve immediately.

VARIATION: Three-quarters of a pound of meadow mushrooms, hens-of-the-woods, or chanterelles may be substituted for the oysters and boletes. If you have no mushroom liquid available increase the milk to ¾ cup.

◇   ◇   ◇

Warm Oyster Mushroom and Pasta Salad with Goat Cheese Dressing

Some food pairings seem to have been made in heaven. Certainly pasta and wild mushrooms is one of them. In this lovely dish the shape of the agnolotti echoes the shape of the mushrooms, while the crunchy texture and astringency of the marinated onions provide a pleasant contrast to the creamy smoothness of the oyster mushrooms.

Your produce store may occasionally have a cluster of very young oyster mushrooms appearing to grow out of a thick mass of stems. These young mushrooms are what the Japanese call mukurojitake or shimeji, and they are particularly tasty. If you come across them, by all means use them in this recipe. The stems also have a lot of flavor. If they are still moist and not woody, they can be sautéed or added to sauces.

This dish has its roots in California cuisine. Serve at room temperature.

Serves 6 as first course
     4 as a main course

1 pound small oyster mushrooms
1 small or ½ medium Bermuda onion, trimmed, peeled, and cut into large dice
1 teaspoon sugar
2 tablespoons balsamic vinegar or good-quality red wine vinegar
1 tablespoon water
3 tablespoons green extra virgin olive oil
3 tablespoons unsalted butter
¾ cup crème fraîche (page 194)

3 ounces imported goat cheese
2 ounces grated Parmesan cheese
1 pound fresh agnolotti pasta

1. Wipe the mushrooms clean with a damp cloth or brush and trim. If the caps are large, slice them thick. Set aside.
2. Blanch the diced onion for 20 seconds in boiling water. Drain.
3. Combine the sugar, vinegar, and water in a small saucepan and bring to a boil. Add the onion, lower the heat, cover, and simmer 3 to 4 minutes. Drain and set aside.
4. Heat the oil and butter in a large skillet. When the butter has melted, add the mushrooms and cook over moderate heat until they begin to color, about 5 or 6 minutes. Lower the heat, add the crème fraîche, and cook, stirring occasionally, for 8 minutes or until the cream is reduced by half and is thick enough to coat the mushrooms.
5. Meanwhile, cook the pasta al dente. Drain. Combine the pasta and the onions with the mushrooms in the skillet, sprinkle with the goat cheese and the Parmesan, and cook 1 minute longer, tossing gently to blend. Transfer to a serving bowl and allow to cool slightly before serving.
VARIATION: Boletes or meadow mushrooms would make interesting substitutes in this recipe.

◇   ◇   ◇

Oyster Mushroom and Rabbit Stew

This fragrant melange of mushrooms and rabbit is particularly toothsome when teamed with cornmeal. Grits, cornmeal mush, soufflé, or polenta are excellent accompaniments.

Serves 4

1 pound oyster mushrooms
  Freshly squeezed juice of ½ lemon
1 tablespoon green extra virgin olive oil
4 tablespoons unsalted butter
2- to 3-pound dressed rabbit, preferably fresh
  (not frozen), cut into serving pieces
1 sprig fresh rosemary, or ¼ teaspoon dried
1 slice thick-sliced bacon, diced
1 clove garlic, minced
1 medium onion, chopped
1 tablespoon flour
½ cup good red wine, such as a Bordeaux
⅔ cup rich chicken stock (page 192), or canned chicken
  broth
½ teaspoon kosher salt
⅛ teaspoon freshly ground black pepper
1 tablespoon chopped fresh mint or 1 teaspoon dried

1.   Wipe the mushrooms with a damp cloth or brush. Cut the caps into thin slices, place them in a large bowl, sprinkle with the lemon juice, and toss. Set aside.
2.   Heat the oil and 2 tablespoons of the butter in a large heavy-bottomed skillet for which you have a cover. Add the rabbit and the rosemary. Brown the rabbit on both sides over moderate heat. Remove the meat with a slotted spoon and keep it warm.

3.   Remove and discard rosemary. Draw off all but 1 tablespoon of the fat in the pan. Add the mushrooms and the lemon juice, cover, and cook over low heat for 5 minutes, stirring occasionally. Remove the cover and continue cooking until the liquid has evaporated. Add the remaining 2 tablespoons butter, bacon, garlic, and onion to the pan and sauté for 5 minutes, stirring occasionally. Return the rabbit to the skillet, sprinkle it with the flour, and cook 2 minutes longer, stirring occasionally. Add the wine and continue stirring until the sauce begins to thicken. Add the stock, salt, and pepper, stir well, cover, and cook over low heat for 30 minutes.

4.   Transfer the rabbit to a serving platter, spoon the sauce over it, and garnish with the mint. Serve immediately.

NOTE: If fresh rabbits are not available, dressed rabbits can be found in the frozen food section of almost all supermarkets. If you use a frozen rabbit be sure to defrost it thoroughly in the refrigerator before cooking. If rabbit is not to your liking you may substitute skinned chicken parts.

VARIATION: Any wild mushroom or combination of mushrooms may be substituted for the oysters.

◇   ◇   ◇

HEDGEHOG
MUSHROOMS

GENUS: *Hydnum* or *Dentinum*

SPECIES: *repandum*

COMMON NAMES: Hedgehog, Sweet Tooth, Wood Urchin (Eng.); Pied-de-Mouton, Barbe-de-Chèvre (Fr.); Semmel-Stopelpilz (Ger.); Steccherino d'orato (It.); Kolczak Oblaczasty (Pol.)

MARKET AVAILABILITY: In good years they are available from August through December

◇   ◇   ◇

Hedgehogs grow in practically all areas of the country, though not always in large numbers. Their favorite habitat is the ground under hardwoods, conifers, and mixed woods. Another species, not often found in food shops, but equally tasty, is the "kissing cousin" of the hedgehog (the *Dentinum umbilicatum*). This smaller mushroom prefers swamps and bogs. Yet despite the difference in their natural environments they are both treats to eat.

As fungi go, the hedgehog is strangely endearing. Its wavy, yellow orange cap is irregularly shaped and sits a bit off center on a smooth, white, rather thick stem. Instead of pores or gills, hedgehogs sport white teeth that resemble tiny, soft-sculpture stalactites. The total effect is of a slightly drunk, perpetually off-balance gnome wearing a floppy hat.

This mild but very flavorful mushroom is an old friend to French and Italian cooks, but up to now it has only rarely made an appearance in American markets.

When buying Hedgehogs, look for specimens that have

smooth caps as moist to the touch as cultivated supermarket mushrooms. Their thick, soft flesh tends to be very brittle, so finding an unbroken specimen in a store is no mean feat. But don't despair, a broken hedgehog tastes just as sweet.

Clean them gently. Their teeth need not be cleaned but their caps and stems should be wiped with a damp cloth.

Mushroom-Herb Bread

Once homemade bread was as common as the cold, but in today's world of small kitchens and working couples, it is a luxury rarely enjoyed. Here is a superb homemade loaf that is so easy to prepare (it needs no kneading) and so uniquely delicious you will make it often.

Makes one loaf

½ pound hedgehog mushrooms
2 tablespoons vegetable oil
3 cloves garlic, minced
1 tablespoon chopped fresh thyme
  or 1 teaspoon dried
1 tablespoon chopped fresh rosemary
  or 1 teaspoon dried
  Salt
3 cups whole wheat flour
2 teaspoons kosher salt
1 package dry yeast
3 tablespoons dark brown sugar
2 generous tablespoons molasses
1½ cups hot, not scalding, water

1. Wipe the mushrooms clean with a damp cloth or mushroom brush and trim the bases of the stems. Cut them into large dice and set aside.

2. Heat the oil in a medium-sized skillet over low heat, add the garlic, and cook, stirring, 30 seconds. Add the mushrooms, toss, and cook until all their liquid has evaporated. Remove the pan from the heat and sprinkle in the thyme and rosemary. Salt lightly and set aside to cool.

3. Mix together the flour, kosher salt, yeast, and brown sugar in a large glass or ceramic bowl, add the molasses, water and mushrooms and stir until the flour is completely moistened. Beat the dough about 40 strokes with a wooden spoon. The batter will be very thick and moist.

4. Generously grease the bottom and sides of a 10-inch springform pan. Turn the dough into the pan, wet your hands slightly, and press the dough out to the edges of the pan with your fingers. Cover the pan with a dish towel and place in a warm place to rise until it has doubled in size, about 30 minutes.

5. Preheat oven to 375° while bread is rising.

6. Bake the bread in the middle of the preheated oven for 35 minutes or until a cake tester comes out clean when inserted in the center. Remove the pan from the oven and allow it to cool for 10 minutes. Run a sharp knife around the sides of the pan and release the spring before removing the loaf. Cool the bread completely on a wire rack before slicing.

VARIATION: A combination of mushrooms such as chanterelles, oysters, and shiitakes may also be used with excellent results.

Hedgehog and Hazelnut Soup

Nut-flavored soups are as old as the Middle Ages and as new as American cuisine.

Serves 4 to 6

  1 pound hedgehog mushrooms
  3 slices dried boletes, broken into small pieces
  3 heads Boston lettuce, tough outer leaves removed
  4 tablespoons unsalted butter
  ½ teaspoon sugar
  1 teaspoon kosher salt
    Freshly ground black pepper
  1 large onion, peeled and quartered
  5 cups rich chicken stock (page 192)
4¼ cups whole milk
  ½ cup cooked white rice
  6 ounces hazelnuts, blanched and skinned
  3 egg yolks, beaten
  ¼ cup heavy cream

1.   Wipe the hedgehog mushrooms clean with a damp cloth or brush and trim the bases of the stems. Coarsely chop mushrooms and set aside.
2.   Wash the dried boletes pieces quickly under running cold water to remove any grit, pat them dry, and set aside.
3.   Remove the core of each head of lettuce. Wash the leaves thoroughly, shake to remove excess water, and shred. (The leaves should not be completely dry.) Set aside.
4.   Melt 2 tablespoons of butter in a large saucepan or stockpot. Add the hedgehogs, toss, and cook 1 minute, stirring. Add the lettuce leaves, sugar, salt, and pepper. Stir once or twice to mix, cover, and cook over moderately low heat for 20 minutes, stirring occasionally.

5. Combine the onion, stock, 4 cups of the milk, rice, and bolete pieces and add them to the pot. Stir once or twice to blend, then cover the pot and simmer over low heat for 1 hour.

6. Strain the soup, reserving the vegetables. Purée the vegetables in a blender or food processor fitted with the metal blade, then combine purée with soup and return it to the pot. Bring the soup back to a simmer.

7. In a food processor fitted with the metal blade, finely chop the hazelnuts. Add the remaining 2 tablespoons of butter and pulse the machine on and off 4 times. Add the remaining ¼ cup milk, the egg yolks, and cream, then pulse the machine 3 more times to mix thoroughly. Add a little of the hot soup to the processor bowl to warm the nut cream, then stir the warm nut cream into the soup. Serve immediately.

VARIATION: Any mild-flavored mushroom such as young oyster or meadow mushrooms may be substituted for the hedgehogs.

Hedgehog, Leek, and Cheese Quiche

The speed with which fashions in food change has left many a casualty in its wake. The quiche is one such victim. Like a designer dress whose purloined copies are now sold off the rack, it has been declared less than chic by the trendsetters. Yet quiche is a superb medium for the woodsy flavor of mushrooms and so, despite the dictums of the food mavens, I recommend you try this uniquely flavored vegetable pie. You may find that it becomes a seasonal favorite in your home.

Serves 6

Pastry for a 9-inch open-face pie (page 195)
¾ cup grated sharp Cheddar cheese
½ pound hedgehog mushrooms
4 young leeks, trimmed
3 tablespoons unsalted butter
1 tablespoon finely chopped pickled jalapeño
 pepper, or more, to taste
1 tablespoon chopped roasted red pepper
 or canned pimiento
 Pinch nutmeg
 Pinch cayenne
3 whole eggs
⅓ cup whole milk
⅓ cup sour cream
⅛ teaspoon kosher salt

1. Preheat oven to 375°.
2. Line a 9-inch pie pan with the pastry and flute the edges. Sprinkle the bottom of the crust with ½ of the grated Cheddar cheese and set aside.
3. Wipe the mushrooms clean with a damp cloth and trim the bases of the stems. Chop the mushrooms into large pieces and set aside.
4. Wash the leeks thoroughly under cold running water, pat dry, then slice them into 2-inch-long matchstick strips. (Use the white part of the leek and ½ inch of the green part.) Set aside.
5. Melt the butter in a large nonstick skillet, add the leeks, and sauté over moderate heat until just tender. Add the mushrooms and cook, stirring, until all the mushroom liquid has evaporated. Add the chopped peppers, nutmeg,

and cayenne. Remove the pan from the heat and allow the vegetables to cool to tepid.

6.   Meanwhile, combine the eggs, milk, sour cream, and salt and whisk them together to make a custard.

7.   Spread the mushrooms and leeks evenly over the cheese in the pie pan, cover with the remaining cheese, and carefully pour in the custard. Bake in the preheated oven for 25 minutes or until a cake tester inserted in the center of the pie comes out clean. Serve hot or cold.

VARIATION: Any fresh mushroom may be substituted for the hedgehogs.

Spicy Scrambled Eggs with Mushrooms

(Huevos Rancheros con Hongos)

Although wild mushrooms are not frequently found in Mexican markets, they are, when available, highly prized. As a child growing up in Mexico, I was sometimes taken to the vegetable market in Xochimilco, a city better known for its "floating gardens" than for its food. During the rainy season, it was a veritable cornucopia of wild mushrooms. Later, if I behaved, I would be treated by our cook to my favorite huevos rancheros con hongos. *This was often incentive enough to prevent me from climbing my favorite tree—that day. These are delicious served with hot corn tortillas on the side.*

Serves 4

6 ounces hedgehog mushrooms
2 tablespoons vegetable oil
1 large onion, finely chopped
1 teaspoon chopped pickled jalapeño peppers

1 large sweet red pepper, seeded, and sliced into thin
   strips lengthwise
1 large sweet green pepper, seeded, and sliced into thin
   strips lengthwise
4 small tomatoes, peeled, cut in half widthwise, seeded,
   and each half cut into quarters
2 small cloves garlic, minced
   Salt and freshly ground pepper to taste
2 tablespoons light cream or whole milk
6 large eggs, beaten
1 tablespoon chopped fresh coriander or parsley
   Mild salsa verde de tomatillos (see Note)

1.   Wipe the mushrooms clean with a damp cloth, trim
the bases of the stems, and chop coarse. Set aside.

2.   Heat the oil in a well-seasoned cast-iron skillet or
heavy-bottomed stainless steel skillet, add the onions,
jalapeño peppers, red and green pepper strips, and the
reserved mushrooms. Cook over moderate heat, stirring,
until the onions and peppers begin to soften. Add the
tomatoes and garlic, toss to mix, and season with salt and
freshly ground pepper to taste. Lower the heat and cook,
stirring occasionally, for 5 minutes.

3.   Beat the light cream or milk into the eggs and add to the
skillet. Cook, stirring continuously, until the eggs reach the
consistency you prefer. Correct seasoning and turn out
onto heated plates or a serving platter. Sprinkle with the
chopped coriander. Pass the tomatillo sauce separately.

NOTE: Salsa verde de tomatillos can be purchased in
most supermarkets or hispanic food stores. Use the mildest
form you can get so as not to overpower the flavor of the
mushrooms.

VARIATION: Almost any mushroom can be used
instead of the hedgehogs. The bolder the flavor of the

mushroom, the more jalapeño pepper may be added, or smaller quantities of mushrooms can be used in combination with a mild-flavored mushroom.

Hedgehogs and Oysters Mont d'Or

This contemporary variation on the classical French Mont d'Or is a glorious mound of creamy potatoes hiding, just below its surface, a cache of surprising flavors.

Serves 4 to 6

¾ pound hedgehog mushrooms
2 pounds baking potatoes, peeled and cut into eighths
2 medium onions, peeled and trimmed
6 tablespoons unsalted butter
1 cup light cream, or ½ cup cream mixed with ½ cup milk
3 tender inner stalks celery with leaves, finely minced
1 clove garlic, minced
2 tablespoons cornstarch
3 tablespoons chopped flat parsley
1 teaspoon dried rosemary
    Salt and freshly ground black pepper to taste
2 teaspoons freshly squeezed lemon juice
2 dozen shucked oysters and their liquid
1 tablespoon melted unsalted butter

1. Wipe the mushrooms clean with a damp cloth and trim the bases of the stems. Chop them coarse and set aside.
2. Place the potatoes and one onion, cut into quarters,

in a medium-sized saucepan and cover with cold water. Bring the water to a boil and cook 15 minutes or until the potatoes are tender. Drain. Mash the potatoes and onion in a potato ricer or a food mill, or place in the large bowl of an electric mixer. Add 2 tablespoons of butter cut into small pieces and blend. Beat until the butter is incorporated. Gradually add 4 tablespoons of the cream and continue beating only until the potatoes are completely smooth. Salt lightly and keep warm.

3.   Preheat the oven to 375°.

4.   Chop the remaining onion and combine it with the minced celery and garlic. Melt the remaining 4 tablespoons butter in a heavy-bottomed saucepan, add the vegetables, and cook over moderate heat until they are soft. Add the mushrooms and cook, stirring occasionally, for 10 minutes or until all the liquid has evaporated. Sprinkle in the cornstarch, parsley, and rosemary and stir to blend completely. Add the remaining ¾ cup cream and cook until it begins to thicken. Season with salt and pepper to taste. Remove from the heat and stir occasionally to prevent a skin from forming while you prepare the oysters.

5.   Combine the lemon juice with the oysters and their liquid in a saucepan. Bring the liquid to a boil and cook only until the edges of the oysters begin to curl. Drain and keep warm.

6.   Place the mushroom mixture on the bottom of an attractive ovenproof baking or soufflé dish. Arrange the oysters on top of the vegetables. Spoon the potatoes on top so that the oysters are completely covered. Drizzle the potatoes with the melted butter and place in the preheated oven until the potatoes begin to brown slightly and the vegetables and oysters are heated through, about 3 to 4 minutes. Serve immediately.

VARIATIONS: Chanterelles, boletes, morels, or any of these combined with oyster mushrooms may be used instead of hedgehogs.

Sautéed Sweetbreads and Green Tomatoes with Hedgehog Purée

Save this extremely rich but incredibly delicious dish for a time when you feel like splurging on calories. It will be well worth the indulgence.

Serves 4

2 pairs sweetbreads
1 pound hedgehog mushrooms
½ cup unsalted butter
3 tablespoons flour
½ cup heavy cream
½ cup whole milk
1 teaspoon sea salt
  Generous pinch freshly ground white pepper
2 tablespoons Madeira wine
1 large egg, beaten
¼ cup fine bread crumbs seasoned with a pinch each of dried oregano, sage, and rosemary, and a generous pinch each of kosher salt and freshly ground black pepper
2 large green tomatoes, peeled

1. Soak the sweetbreads in ice cold water to cover for 45 minutes. Drain. Simmer them in acidulated water to cover

15 to 20 minutes or until they turn white. Remove the sweetbreads from the water and immediately submerge them in ice water to cool. Drain, and remove the membrane and connective tissues. Pat dry.

2.   While the sweetbreads are soaking, make the mushroom purée. Wipe the mushrooms with a damp cloth or brush and trim the bases of their stems. Cut approximately ¼ pound of the mushrooms into thin slices and set aside. Cut or break the remaining mushrooms into quarters and reserve separately.

3.   Make a béchamel: Melt 2 tablespoons of the butter over low heat in a small nonstick saucepan. Sprinkle the flour into the pan and stir until you have a completely smooth paste. Combine the cream with the milk and add it to the paste a little at a time, stirring continuously. Do not allow any lumps to form. Cook, stirring continuously, until the béchamel thickens. Add the salt and white pepper and stir to mix. Remove the pan from the heat and set aside.

4.   Combine half of the quartered mushrooms and the Madeira in the bowl of a food processor fitted with the metal blade, and process until the mushrooms are finely chopped. Add half the béchamel and the remaining quartered mushrooms. Continue processing until the mushrooms are puréed, then pour in the remaining béchamel and pulse on and off 3 times to mix. Set aside.

5.   Melt 3 tablespoons of the butter in a large skillet over low heat, then add the reserved sliced mushrooms and sauté, stirring, until they have given up their liquid. Turn the mushroom purée into the skillet and cook, stirring continuously, about 5 minutes or until the purée is thick enough to coat a spoon. Remove from the heat and keep warm while you prepare the sweetbreads.

6.   Divide each sweetbread in half. Dip each half in beaten egg and roll it in the seasoned breadcrumbs to coat.

7.   Heat the remaining 3 tablespoons butter in a nonstick skillet until it begins to bubble. Add the sweetbreads and fry them over moderate heat until they are nicely browned on both sides. Remove them from the skillet and keep warm.

8.   Cut each tomato crosswise into six slices. In the same skillet you used to sautée the sweetbreads, fry the tomato slices on both sides over moderate heat until tender, adding a little butter to the pan if necessary.

9.   To serve, arrange 3 overlapping slices of tomatoes on each plate. Rest one half sweetbread partially on the edge of the tomatoes. Spoon the mushroom purée on the plate around the sweetbread.

VARIATION: Young oyster mushrooms, meadow mushrooms, or the tender edges of hens-of-the-woods may be substituted for the hedgehogs.

CHICKEN-*of-the*-WOODS
and
HEN-*of-the*-WOODS

GENUS: *Polyporus*
SPECIES: *sulphureus*
COMMON NAMES: Chicken-of-the-Woods, Chicken mushroom (Eng.); Polypore soufre (Fr.);
Schwefel-porling (Ger.); Poliporo sulfureo (it.); Zolciak siarkowy (Pol.)
GENUS: *Grifola* (formerly *Polyporus*)
SPECIES: *frondosa*
COMMON NAMES: Hen-of-the-Woods (Eng.); Poule de Bois, Polypore-en-tuffe, Pied-de-griffon (Fr.);
Laubporling, Klapperschwamm (Ger.); Grifo (It.);
Zagwica listkowata (Pol.)
MARKET AVAILABILITY: In some years as early as June, but more often in the fall

◇   ◇   ◇

Chicken-of-the-woods and hen-of-the-woods are two of the most spectacular mushrooms found in shops today. We call them mushrooms but, of course, they're not the cap-on-stem fungi we usually have in mind when we say mushroom.

Chicken-of-the-woods is most often found on logs, stumps, or tree trunks of a large variety of hardwoods and conifers, where it grows in large clusters of stalkless bright orange or brilliant yellow velvety caps that overlap each other. Occasionally, it appears on the ground, growing from a single stalk. This showy fungus can be found throughout the United States in abundance in late summer and through the fall. Its caps range in size from 6 to 12 inches across.

The chicken-of-the-woods's flavor is strong and slightly resiny with the merest hint of bitters. Its thick, firm flesh is soft at the edges and gets tougher as it nears the center. The soft edges of young caps make the best eating, but since shops often offer only pieces that have been cut from larger caps, it's sometimes difficult to tell simply by sight which caps are young and which are past their prime. Avoid older caps that feel woody or rubbery. However, you may find that you have to buy some of the less tender parts of the cap in order to get the tender edges. Provided they aren't woody, these tougher portions can be sliced thin and used in stews. They make a great addition to any long-cooking dish.

The hen-of-the-woods can be found near stumps of oaks or other hardwoods, its darkly tipped silvery fronds folded over one another like the feathers of a sitting hen protecting its nest. This magnificent and sometimes gigantic fungus grows wild in the eastern United States in the fall. The Japanese cultivate it for its excellent culinary properties.

The hen-of-the-woods's flavor is less assertive than that of the "chicken's," but no less appealing. Its flesh is crisper and more fragile and therefore requires less cooking time.

Coming upon these gorgeous fungi in the woods is terribly exciting because of their size. But it is no less exciting to encounter them in shops. I saw a "hen" in a local shop recently that weighed over eighteen pounds. I bought only two of its delicious fronds. The next day I returned to purchase more only to be told that a caterer had bought all but my two fronds. From now on, I buy in quantity.

Chicken-of-the-Woods Chips
with Trout Pâté

We've had potato chips, taco chips, banana chips, even "shrimp chips," why not mushroom chips?

Served with smoked trout pâté, deep-fried chicken-of-the woods chips make a unique and beautiful first course. The trick is to produce very thin large slices. To do this it is useful to use a food processor fitted with a very thin slicing disc, a truffle slicer, or the slicing blade of a hand grater.

Serves 4 as a first course

   1 pound firm chicken-of-the-woods caps
     Oil for deep-frying
     Salt to taste
   2 smoked trout weighing about ¾ pound total, skinned and filleted
   6 ounces cream cheese, at room temperature
   2 ounces unsalted butter, at room temperature
1½ tablespoons prepared white horseradish
1½ tablespoons chopped capers
     Chopped fresh chervil (if not available, use parsley)

1.   Wipe the mushroom caps with a damp cloth or brush and trim the tough ends. Using tweezers, remove any pine needles or grass that may be embedded in the caps.

2.   Starting at the soft edge of the cap and working toward the center, cut as many very thin slices from the cap as possible. If you are using a food processor, fit it with the thinnest slicing disc. Cut the caps into sizes that will fit the feeder tube and position them so that the disc will cut into the soft edge of the cap first. Process and pat the slices dry.

3.   Heat the oil in a deep-fryer or deep saucepan. When it is bubbling add the mushroom chips a few at a time. Fry until crisp. Remove the chips from the hot oil and place them on several layers of paper towels; salt them very lightly. Repeat the process until all the mushroom slices are fried. When they are completely cooled, they may be stored in an airtight container.

4.   Break up the trout fillets with your fingers. Be certain that all the bones, no matter how small, have been removed. Place the fish in a food processor fitted with the metal blade and process 30 seconds.

5.   Cut the cream cheese and butter into 1-inch cubes and add to the fish. Process 2 to 3 minutes, or until the mixture is quite creamy. Add the horseradish and process an additional 30 seconds. Turn the pâté into a bowl, add the capers, and beat with a wire whisk to blend.

6.   Fit a pastry bag with a straight tube and fill it with the fish pâté. Pipe the pâté equally into each of four ramekins. Cover the ramekins with wax paper and refrigerate for at least 2 hours (overnight is preferable).

7.   To serve, set each ramekin on individual serving dishes. Sprinkle the top of the pâté with chopped chervil and surround the ramekins with generous helpings of mushroom chips. Pass a pepper mill separately.

NOTE: Smoked bluefish may be substituted for the trout. If you use bluefish, omit the horseradish and add 2 teaspoons freshly squeezed lemon juice instead.

◇   ◇   ◇

Chicken-of-the-Woods Chicken Salad

Chicken-of-the-woods adds remarkable flavor and just the right touch of fall color to this perfect tailgate picnic salad. It is elegant enough for champagne and robust enough for beer. Serve this on a bed of red leaf lettuce.

Serves 4 to 6

8 ounces chicken-of-the-woods caps
2 tablespoons unsalted butter
1 tablespoon extra virgin olive oil (preferably Italian)
1 medium onion, chopped
1 sun-dried tomato, drained and cut into thin strips
1 tablespoon good red wine, such as Bordeaux
Salt and freshly ground black pepper
1½ to 2 pounds cooked chicken, skinned, boned, and cut into large chunks
3 thick slices bacon, fried crisp, drained, and crumbled
½ cup pecan halves
2½ tablespoons chopped fresh dill or 1 teaspoon dry
1½ cups cooked brown rice
Champagne Vinaigrette (see recipe below)

1. Wipe the mushrooms with a damp cloth or brush. Trim away the tough bases or any blemishes. Remove any grass that may be embedded in the caps. Slice the caps about ¹⁄₁₆ inch thick.
2. Melt the butter in a skillet and add the oil. Add the onion and tomato and cook, stirring, until the onion is soft. Do not allow it to color. Add the mushrooms and

wine, season very lightly with salt and pepper, and sauté, stirring occasionally, over moderate heat for 5 minutes.

3. Add the chicken, bacon, nuts, dill, and rice and toss to mix. Cool. Sprinkle with vinaigrette to taste and chill.

CHAMPAGNE VINAIGRETTE

¼ cup champagne vinegar (see note)
½ teaspoon kosher salt
⅛ teaspoon freshly ground black pepper
1 teaspoon Dijon-style mustard
1 teaspoon sugar
½ cup extra virgin olive oil

Combine the vinegar, salt, pepper, mustard, and sugar in a screw-top jar. Close tightly and shake 30 seconds or until the salt and sugar are dissolved. Add the olive oil, close tightly, and shake vigorously for 1 minute.

NOTE: If champagne vinegar is not available, a good quality white wine vinegar will do. If the sauce is not used immediately, the oil will separate. Shake again just before using.

VARIATION: Very small chanterelles may be used instead of the "chickens."

◇   ◇   ◇

Chicken-of-the-Woods and Potato Tart

In this version of the classic French Tarte de Pommes de Terre, chicken-of-the-woods supplies a touch of unexpected color and a good deal of provocative flavor.

Serves 6 to 8

    1 pound chicken-of-the-woods caps
      Pastry for a 2-crust pie (page 195)
1½ pounds baking potatoes
    1 egg yolk
    1 tablespoon cream
    3 thick slices cured bacon, about 3 ounces
    1 medium onion, chopped
    1 tablespoon chopped parsley
1¼ teaspoons kosher salt
      Freshly ground black pepper
    ¼ cup sour cream
    ¼ cup heavy cream
    1 teaspoon chopped fresh lemon thyme or ¼
      teaspoon dried thyme

1. Wipe the mushrooms with a damp cloth or brush. Remove any grass or pine needles that may be embedded in the caps. Trim away the tough bases and cut the caps into 1½-inch-long julienne strips. Set aside.

2. Roll out ⅔ of the pie dough to a thickness of ⅛ inch. Line an 11-inch tart pan with the dough. Cover the pan with plastic wrap and refrigerate. Roll the remaining ⅓ of the dough into a circle large enough to cover the tart with 1 inch to spare. Cover the circle of dough with a sheet of

plastic wrap, then fold it in half and wrap in plastic wrap. Refrigerate the dough until needed.

3.   Peel the potatoes, cut them in half crosswise, and put them in cold water to cover. Set aside.

4.   Preheat the oven to 375°.

5.   To make a glaze for the crust, whisk together the egg yolk and 1 tablespoon cream in a small bowl. Cover with plastic wrap and refrigerate.

6.   Dice the bacon. In a heavy-bottomed skillet, sauté the bacon over low heat until it is translucent. Add the onion and continue to cook, stirring, until it is soft. Add the mushrooms, toss, and cook for 5 minutes or until all the liquid in the pan has evaporated.

7.   Drain the potatoes and place them, cut side down, in a food processor fitted with the thinnest slicing disk. The potato slices should be paper-thin, as for chips. Arrange half of the potato slices in overlapping circles in the bottom of the lined tart pan. Sprinkle with half of the parsley, 3/4 teaspoon of the salt, and several grindings of fresh pepper. Gently, so as not to disturb the potato arrangement, spread the mushroom mixture evenly over the potatoes. Mix sour cream and heavy cream in a small bowl. Pour on half of the cream, then arrange the remaining potatoes over the mushrooms. Sprinkle with the remaining parsley, salt, and additional grindings of pepper. Pour on the remaining cream, and sprinkle with thyme.

8.   Remove the folded dough from the refrigerator. Peel off the outer sheet of plastic wrap and let the dough stand at room temperature for 5 to 7 minutes. Unfold the pastry and remove the inner sheet of plastic wrap. Refold the pastry, then with a sharp knife cut four 1-inch arrowhead shapes along the fold.

9.   Turn the pastry out over half of the tart, leaving 1 inch

overhanging the edge, then unfold the second half. Fold the 1-inch overhang back toward the center of the tart so that you have a triple thickness of dough around the rim of the pan. Press the edges of the pastry together to seal and brush the top with the prepared glaze.

10.   Bake in the center of the preheated oven until the potatoes are thoroughly cooked (they should feel soft when pierced with a cake tester or skewer) and the crust is golden brown. Cool on a rack for 10 minutes before serving.

VARIATION: Shiitakes, hens-of-the-woods, chanterelles, or meadows may be substituted for the "chickens." Be sure to slice the mushrooms thin. The shiitakes and chanterelles may be cut into julienne strips.

Hen-of-the-Woods Custard Soup

(MAITAKE CHAWAN MUSHI)

The hen-of-the-woods is a particular favorite in Japan where it is called maitake, the dancing mushroom. In Japan maitakes are cultivated commercially and therefore small specimens are often found in supermarkets. We, on the other hand, are still limited to the wildlings found in our forests, which tend to be considerably larger.

Serves 4

   4 clumps of tiny hen-of-the-woods fronds, or 4 small single fronds
2½ cups rich chicken stock (page 192) or canned chicken broth
   8 small shrimp, shelled, deveined and split lengthwise
   1 tablespoon mirin (see note) or cocktail sherry

1 tablespoon soy sauce
4 large eggs
1 freshly roasted or canned chestnut, cut into
   quarters
4 sprigs fresh coriander, chopped

1.   Wipe the mushrooms clean with a damp cloth or brush and trim their bases.
2.   Bring the chicken broth to a boil in a medium-sized saucepan, then lower the heat and add the mushrooms. Cover the pan and simmer 5 minutes. Remove the mushrooms with a slotted spoon and drain. Let the mushrooms and the stock cool to room temperature.
3.   Blanch the shrimp in boiling water just until they turn opaque, then plunge them into ice water to cool. Drain and set aside.
4.   Combine the cooled broth, mirin, and soy sauce and stir to mix thoroughly. In a medium-sized bowl, beat the eggs. While stirring the eggs gently, slowly add the seasoned broth. Do not create bubbles.
5.   Divide the shrimp and chestnut quarters equally among 4 heatproof pots de crème or custard cups. Gently spoon the custard into the cups to about ½ inch from the top. Carefully insert the mushroom fronds in the center of the each cup, sprinkle the surrounding custard with the coriander, and cover tightly with foil. Set the cups in a vegetable steamer and steam about 20 minutes or until the custard has set. Remove the foil and serve.
NOTE: Mirin, a sweet Japanese rice wine, is available in oriental food shops.

◊   ◊   ◊

Hen-of-the-Woods with Snails Sauté

(Poule de bois aux Escargots)

As any forager can tell you, snails love wild mushrooms. Snails and mushrooms are also a natural flavor pairing, as you will taste for yourself in this classy first course dish that's guaranteed to have you asking for more.

Serves 4 as a first course

6 ounces hen-of-the-woods fronds
1 large garlic clove, peeled
2 tablespoons extra virgin olive oil
2 tablespoons chopped fresh parsley
2 tablespoons chopped roasted sweet red pepper
1 tablespoon minced shallots
1 teaspoon anchovy paste
1 tablespoon flour
1 cup dry white wine (I prefer Pouilly-Fuissé but any other good white will do)
Pinch each of nutmeg and cayenne pepper
Salt and freshly ground black pepper to taste
3 egg yolks
2 dozen canned cooked snails, drained
1 tablespoon chopped fresh coriander leaves
Lemon wedges for garnish

1. Wipe the mushrooms with a damp cloth or brush and trim any tough parts if necessary. Chop them fine and set aside.
2. Mash the garlic clove into a paste, cover with plastic wrap, and set aside.
3. Heat the oil in a saucepan. Add the mushrooms and

toss to coat them. Stir in the parsley, pepper, shallots, and reserved garlic paste, and cook the vegetables over low heat for 5 minutes. Stir in the anchovy paste and the flour. Very slowly add the wine, stirring continuously. Add the nutmeg, cayenne, salt and pepper to taste, and simmer, stirring occasionally, for 5 minutes. Remove from the heat.

4.   Stirring rapidly with a wooden spoon, add one egg yolk at a time off heat, incorporating it completely before adding the next. Add the drained snails to the saucepan and return it to low heat. Cook 2 minutes or until the snails are heated through. Garnish with chopped coriander and serve with lemon wedges.

◇   ◇   ◇

Hen-of-the-Woods Rice with Quail Teriyaki

This recipe is a fine example of how many different cuisines combine to produce the new American cuisine. It is elegant, exquisitely flavored, and quite easy to prepare.

Serves 4

- 1 cup short-grain rice
- 3/4 pound hen-of-the-woods mushrooms
- 1/4 pound fresh shiitake mushrooms
- 1 teaspoon vegetable oil
- 2 medium eggs, beaten lightly
- 6 tablespoons mirin, available in oriental food shops
- 4 tablespoons unsalted butter
- 1 large onion, chopped
- 1 carrot, scraped and coarsely chopped
- 2 3/4 cups chicken broth
- 1 teaspoon kosher salt
- 3 tablespoons soy sauce
- 6 tablespoons sake or dry white wine
- 5 teaspoons sugar
- 2 tablespoons rendered chicken fat or clarified butter
- 8 quails, preferably boned, but this is not imperative
- 1/2 sheet *nori* (paper-thin dried Japanese seaweed, available in oriental food shops and some health food shops), cut into 2-inch matchstick strips

1.   Place the rice in cold water to cover and stir until the water turns white. Drain. Repeat this process until the water remains clear. Drain and let the rice stand 30 minutes in a strainer.

2.   Wipe the mushrooms clean with a damp cloth or brush. Trim away the tough portions of the hens-of-the-woods and remove any grass or twigs that may be embedded in the caps. Chop coarsely and set aside. Remove the stems from the shiitakes and discard; slice the caps thin. Set aside.

3.   Wipe a medium-sized nonstick skillet with the vegetable oil and heat. Combine the eggs and 1 tablespoon mirin and blend thoroughly, then add the eggs to the skillet and cook over high heat, shaking the pan back and forth over the burner, until the top of the eggs is dry. Slide the sheet of eggs out onto a damp dish towel and roll it up loosely as for a jelly roll. Set aside.

4.   Melt the butter in a large skillet for which you have a tight-fitting cover. Add the onions and carrots, and sauté over moderate heat just until the onions are tender. Add the mushrooms, toss, and sauté for 5 minutes longer. Stir in the washed rice and cook, stirring occasionally, until the grains turn opaque. Do not allow the rice to brown. Add the broth and salt. Raise the heat to high, bring the broth to a boil, cover the pan tightly, and reduce the heat to low. Simmer the rice for 20 minutes or until all the liquid has been absorbed. Keep warm.

5.   To make the teriyaki sauce, combine the soy sauce, sake, the remaining 5 tablespoons of mirin, and the sugar in a small bowl and stir until the sugar dissolves. Set aside.

6.   Prick the quails all over with a fork and set them aside.

7.   Melt the chicken fat over high heat in a medium-sized skillet for which you have a cover. Lower the heat to medium and add the quails. Brown the birds on all sides, then cover the pan and cook for 7 minutes. Transfer the birds to a heated plate and keep them warm.

8.   Add the teriyaki sauce to the skillet and deglaze the

pan, scraping up any browned bits that are stuck to the bottom or sides. Bring the sauce to a boil over medium heat and cook, stirring, for 2 minutes or until the sauce begins to thicken slightly. Return the birds to the skillet, raise the heat, and continue cooking, turning them several times to coat them with the sauce. Remove the quails when the sauce is reduced by half.

9. To serve, place the quails in the center of a serving platter, breasts up. Arrange the rice around them. Slice the rolled egg into thin circles and arrange the circles over the rice. Sprinkle the rice with the seaweed strips and serve.

NOTE: 2 medium Cornish hens may be substituted for the quail (allow half a hen per serving and reduce the chicken fat to 1 tablespoon).

VARIATION: Oyster mushrooms may be substituted for the hens-of-the-woods.

◇   ◇   ◇

WINTER

Truffles are the only edible fungus harvested in winter. When the first signs of frost appear in France and Italy (where most of the world's truffles are found) trained dogs and pigs begin their search for these precious nodules.

Historically truffles have been sought for their flavor but they have also traditionally been thought to have the power to inflame passions. The venerable Doctor Brillat-Savarin believed that just speaking the word truffle ". . . awakens erotic and gastronomical dreams." As proof of his contention he related, in his celebrated book *The Physiology of Taste,* an incident that occurred in the home of a virtuous married lady of his acquaintance. Displaying great restraint, the lady in question consumed at dinner only the smallest amount of truffle, yet she soon found herself, if not encouraging, clearly not discouraging the increasingly improper advances of the man (not her husband) with whom she had shared her meal. Fortunately for the lady she "awoke . . . as from a dream" and repulsed him. "What can I say, monsieur?" the gentlewoman pleaded, "I blame the whole thing on the truffles."

◇　◇　◇

TRUFFLES

GENUS: *Tuber*

SPECIES: *Melanosporum* and *magnatum*

COMMON NAMES: Périgord truffle, Black truffle, Urbano truffle, White truffle (Eng.); Truffe (Fr.); Tartufo bianco (It.); Trufla czarnozarodnikowa (Pol.)

MARKET AVAILABILITY: Fresh truffles begin to appear in specialty shops in December, and are often available through March

◇ ◇ ◇

My husband contends that, in fairness to consumers, truffles should be labeled "Warning: Truffles may be hazardous to your wealth." At a price of about $600 a pound for fresh Périgord truffles and not much less for Urbano white truffles, truffles can't be considered a budget item. Yet while they are pricey, for dedicated gourmets their cost has rarely been a deterrent.

Truffles grow from two to eight inches below the surface of chalky soil at the base of oak and sometimes beech and hazel trees. A fully fruited truffle can vary in size from a large marble to a small baking potato (the latter would be considered quite a find). They are roughly round in shape. The black truffle has a grayish black, rather scaly exterior, but its interior is black and smooth, and marbled with a network of fine white hairlike mycelia throughout. The so-called white (Urbano) truffle is really buff to beige in color on the outside and slightly lighter on the inside.

Truffles are usually hunted with the aid of trained pigs

or dogs since these animals possess an acute sense of smell and are good diggers—characteristics useful in finding truffles. The same strong odor (a steroidal sex attractant called androsterone) that repels uninitiated truffle consumers causes pigs and dogs to head straight to the buried fungi.

In Babylonian times truffles were eaten only by nobility. Later, the Romans imported them at enormous expense from the deserts of North Africa. After the decline of the Roman Empire they were little heard of (according to Ray Tannahill's *Food in History*) until the fourteenth century when they surfaced again in France, this time to be "pickled in vinegar, soaked in hot water, and served with butter."

In 1644 John Evelyn tells us in his diary that while stopping in Vienne in the Dauphin he "supp'd; having (amongst other dainties) a dish of Truffles, which is a certaine earth nut. . . ." Always a man of elevated taste and intelligence, he goes on to say, "It is in truth an incomparable meate. . . ."

In 1737 William Byrd of Virginia, hoping to sell a large tract of his land to a Swiss religious group, wrote for his prospective buyers *A Natural History of Virginia, or The Newly Discovered Eden.* In it he describes Virginia's abundant wild and cultivated flora and fauna. Under what he called "Pot Herbs" he lumped together such items as cabbage, artichokes, horseradish and "many species of potatoes, also truffles. . . ."

Back in France, Brillat-Savarin tells us in *The Physiology of Taste,* that "truffles were rare in Paris (in) 1780 . . . a truffled turkey was a luxurious item which could be seen only on the tables of the highest nobility or the best-paid whores." However, by 1825 when his book was published, things had changed. "No man would dare assert that he had dined at table where at least one truffled dish was wanting." He credited their widespread availability to "merchants of fine edibles" who, seeing that there was a growing market for them, paid high prices to anyone who could find them. Happily, today's "merchants of fine edibles" continue to do the same.

When purchasing fresh truffles, be certain they are quite firm. Soft spots mean decay. Most shops will store fresh truffles buried in rice in a cool place, to keep them dry. If you're not planning to use them immediately, do the same or put them in a screw-top jar, fill it with brandy, vodka, bourbon, or some other high-proof alcoholic beverage and close the jar tightly. They will keep in alcohol for about six weeks. As long as air doesn't get to them their aroma and flavor will not evaporate.

Wipe fresh truffles with a damp cloth or brush, as you would other mushrooms, and peel them with a sharp knife. Save the peelings (in alcohol as indicated above) to use, chopped, in scrambled eggs or in pâtés.

Truffle Omelet

There is perhaps no more elegant way to break fast than with a truffle omelet; however, it also makes a lovely light supper.

Serves 4

1 medium black truffle
2 tablespoons unsalted butter
8 large eggs at room temperature
1 tablespoon cream at room temperature
    Generous pinch table salt

1.   Wipe the truffle clean with a damp cloth and peel. Save the peelings. Cut 4 very thin slices from the center of the truffle and set aside. Mince the remaining truffle and peelings.

2.   Melt 1 tablespoon butter in a small skillet. Add the truffle slices and toss to coat with the butter, then remove the slices and set aside. Add the minced truffle to the skillet and toss to coat, then remove and set aside separately.

3.   In a glass bowl, combine the eggs, cream, and minced truffles and stir very gently with a wire whisk a short time to mix. Do not beat the eggs.

4.   Melt the remaining 1 tablespoon butter in a large, clean nonstick skillet. Tilt the pan to coat it with the butter, then raise the heat to high until a droplet of water added to the skillet sizzles. Pour in the eggs and stir with a wooden or plastic fork twice or three times. Shake the pan so that the eggs cover the bottom and keep shaking the pan to avoid burning the omelet. When the eggs are cooked to your liking (the top should be quite soft), season with the salt and fold the omelet in half. Slide it onto a heated serving plate, garnish with the truffle slices and serve immediately. Pass a pepper mill separately.

When this dish is not served for breakfast, it is traditionally served with a demiglace sauce (see page 46) flavored with Madeira wine.

VARIATION: Horn-of-plenty mushrooms may be used in place of truffles.

◇   ◇   ◇

Cape Cod Bay Scallops with Truffles

Until your rich Aunt Arabelle showers you with "black diamonds" on your birthday, you might want to start small. This dish allows you to decide just how extravagant you wish to be. If you're feeling flush, use 4 small truffles, if it's a while before payday use two, and if you're between jobs, use one and make up the difference with chopped shiitake caps.

This recipe calls for Cape Cod bay or Long Island bay scallops. These are the sweetest varieties and can be found in markets all over the country. They're harvested from November through March but are often available frozen. Freezing causes very little loss of flavor. If you can't find them, use larger scallops and cut them into quarters.

Serves 4

4 black truffles, or 1 or 2 truffles plus 4 large shiitake caps
⅔ pound Cape Cod bay or Long Island bay scallops
½ cup milk
2 sprigs flat-leaf parsley
1 sprig tarragon
Leaves from one inner stalk of celery
1 cup dry white wine
1 medium onion, chopped
1 shallot, minced
6 tablespoons unsalted butter
3 tablespoons flour
4 tablespoons Gruyère cheese
Salt and freshly ground pepper to taste

1.   Wipe the truffles with a damp cloth or brush. Chop and set aside.

2. Combine the scallops and the milk in a small bowl and let stand 3 minutes. Remove the scallops from the milk with a slotted spoon. Strain the milk through a coffee filter and reserve 3 tablespoons.

3. To make a bouquet garni, tie the parsley, tarragon, and celery leaves together with a small piece of kitchen string. In a small saucepan, combine the bouquet garni with the wine, onion, and shallot. Bring the wine to a boil, then reduce the heat and simmer for 10 minutes. Add the scallops to this court bouillon and simmer just until they turn opaque. Do not overcook or they will become rubbery. Remove the scallops to a heated platter with a slotted spoon and keep warm. Strain the court bouillon and reserve.

4. Melt 2 tablespoons of the butter in a nonstick skillet and add the chopped truffles. Sauté over low heat, stirring occasionally, for 3 minutes. Remove the truffles and keep them warm. Melt the remaining 4 tablespoons butter in the skillet, then sprinkle in the flour and stir to blend well. Cook, stirring, for 4 minutes. Do not allow the flour to brown. Stir in the strained court bouillon and reserved 3 tablespoons milk and cook the sauce, stirring, for 5 minutes. Add the scallops and truffles and season to taste. Cook over very low heat an additional 3 minutes, then stir in half the cheese.

5. Mound the scallops and truffles in 8 washed, thoroughly dried, and buttered scallop shells or 4 well-buttered gratin dishes. Sprinkle with the remaining cheese and place under the broiler to brown slightly. Serve immediately.

VARIATION: There is really no substitute for the flavor of truffles; however, chopped horn-of-plenty mushrooms may be substituted for the visual effect only.

Truffled Cornish Hens

This updated version of the truffled turkey on which eighteenth century French nobility and high-priced ladies of the night dined requires a bit of advance preparation. The end product, however, is so spectacular it is well worth the planning.

Serves 4

  2 medium black truffles
¼ cup Cognac
¼ cup tawny port wine
  2 plump cornish hens (about 3½ pounds total)
  4 large shiitake mushrooms
  1 cup canned unsweetened chestnut purée
⅓ pound lean pork, ground
¼ cup bread crumbs
⅛ teaspoon salt
  2 grindings fresh black pepper
  2 tablespoons unsalted butter
  1 carrot, chopped
  1 medium onion, chopped
  1 inner stalk celery with leaves, chopped
    Juice of ½ lemon
  1 slice bacon

1.   Wipe the truffles with a damp cloth and peel. Save the peels for another use. Combine the Cognac and port in a small screw-top jar. Add the truffles, cover tightly, and marinate them for 8 hours.

2.   Taking care not to break the skin, gently run your fingers under the skin of the hens at the breast and the drumsticks to separate it from the meat. Drain the truffles,

reserving the liquor, and cut each one into six slices. Place one slice each under the skin of the upper and lower breast on both sides of the breastbone, and one slice under the skin of each thigh. Cover the hens in plastic wrap and refrigerate overnight.

3.   On the day you plan to serve the hens, wipe the shiitakes with a damp cloth and discard the stems. Chop the caps fine and combine them in a bowl with the chestnut purée, pork, bread crumbs, salt, and pepper. Moisten slightly with 1 tablespoon of the truffle marinade, cover, and refrigerate.

4.   Preheat the oven to 350°.

5.   Melt the butter in a skillet. Add the carrots, onion, and celery, and cook, stirring, over moderate heat until the vegetables are tender. Transfer them to a small roasting pan just large enough to hold the hens.

6.   Rub the cavity of each bird with half of the lemon juice and fill loosely with the shiitake stuffing. Close the cavity with skewers and kitchen thread, and arrange the hens, breast up, on top of the vegetables. Place one-half slice of bacon over each breast and roast the birds in the preheated oven for 30 minutes. Remove the bacon and allow the breasts to brown an additional 15 minutes or until done. Let the birds stand 5 minutes before carving.

NOTE: I have prepared this dish using pitted prunes instead of truffles and it has been quite successful; however, it is in no way the *same* dish.

VARIATION: Small, cleaned, trimmed and halved horns-of-plenty may be substituted for the *color* of the truffles only.

◇   ◇   ◇

Sweet Pepper and White Truffle Salad

This colorful composed salad with its robust Piedmont bagna cauda *sauce is a perfect setting for the flavor of white truffles. Play with the amount of garlic in the sauce, if you like. You may even wish to add some crème fraîche. Doing so would in no way compromise its authenticity.*

Serves 4

1 medium white truffle
4 to 5 large red or yellow sweet peppers, or a combination
2 large ripe tomatoes, peeled
4 small new potatoes, cooked and peeled
½ fennel bulb, trimmed and thinly sliced
  Mixed salad greens

BAGNA CAUDA SAUCE

4 cloves garlic
6 anchovy fillets, rinsed in cold water, patted dry, and chopped
1 cup unsalted butter
4 tablespoons extra virgin olive oil
  Salt to taste

1. Wipe the truffle with a damp cloth or brush. Peel, if necessary, and set aside.

2. Cut the peppers in half lengthwise and remove the seeds and ribs. Roast them under the broiler until their skins are black, then place them in a paper bag for 5 minutes in order to make them easier to peel. Slip the skins off the peppers and cut them into strips. Set aside.

3. Slice the tomatoes and the cooked potatoes and set them aside separately at room temperature.

4. Make the sauce: Mince the garlic in the bowl of a food processor fitted with a metal blade. Add the chopped anchovies and pulse 2 or 3 times to mince. Heat the butter and oil in a small saucepan just until the butter melts. With the processor on, pour the butter/oil mixture through the feed tube a little at a time. Transfer the sauce to the top part of a double boiler, place the pan directly on the heating element, and cook over low heat, stirring with a wooden spoon, for 5 minutes or until the garlic is soft and the anchovies are dissolved. Add salt to taste (remember, anchovies are salty). Remove the pan from the heat and keep warm over hot, not boiling, water.

5. Shave the truffle as thinly as possible. Arrange the peppers, tomatoes, potatoes, and fennel on a bed of salad greens. Spoon the sauce generously over the vegetables, garnish with truffle slices, and serve immediately.

NOTE: Leftover sauce may be brought to the table in a small pan on a warming candle, or refrigerated and reheated very slowly to be served another time as a dip for raw vegetables.

◇   ◇   ◇

Pasta with White Truffles

(PASTA AI TARTUFI)

White truffle cuisine originated in the Piedmont area of Italy where for centuries the trifolau (truffle hunter) would steal out in the middle of the night to dig up his precious "callosities of earth." To hunt by day was to tempt truffle thieves waiting to discover where the treasures were hidden.

The simplicity of this classic pasta insures that nothing will detract from the flavor and aroma of the truffle. Authentic flavor depends on the use of the freshest ingredients—a hallmark of la cucina Piemontese.

Serves 4

  1 large white truffle, about 2 to 3 ounces
½ cup crème fraîche (page 194)
  4 tablespoons unsalted butter
    Salt and freshly ground black pepper
  1 pound very fresh angel hair or other fine pasta

1. Wipe the truffle with a damp brush. Set ¼ of the truffle aside. Cut the remainder of the truffle in half and cut each half into very thin slices.
2. Combine the crème fraîche, butter, and truffle slices in a small saucepan. Cook, stirring, over moderate heat, until the cream is reduced by half. Season with salt and pepper to taste. Set aside.
3. Cook the pasta in boiling, salted water until al dente, 2 or 3 minutes. Drain thoroughly and turn into a serving bowl. Pour the truffle cream over the pasta, toss, grate the reserved ¼ truffle over the surface, and serve immediately. Pass a pepper mill separately.

◇   ◇   ◇

THE ORIENTAL
MUSHROOMS

◇　◇　◇

SHIITAKES

GENUS: *Lentinus*
SPECIES: *edodes*
COMMON NAMES: Golden Oak mushroom, Chinese Black mushroom, Black Forest mushroom (trade name), Doubloon (trade name) (Eng.); Shiitake (Jap.)
MARKET AVAILABILITY: As this is a popular cultivated variety, it is available all year round.

◇   ◇   ◇

The shiitake grows on fallen or cut oak logs both in the wild and when cultivated. Its convex cinnamon brown cap has become a familiar sight in American supermarkets.

Most fresh shiitakes found on produce stands have been cultivated on artificially impregnated oak logs (*shii* meaning a species of oak and *take* meaning mushroom). After button mushrooms, shiitakes are probably the most widely cultivated variety in the world. The Campbell Soup Company, which has successfully cultivated white button mushrooms for years, has begun to cultivate shiitakes for commercial distribution as well. Campbell's is marketing its mushrooms under the name Doubloon in order to differentiate them from those cultivated by other firms such as Phillips Farms in Pennsylvania, who call their shiitakes Black Forest mushrooms. In flavor and texture these American shiitakes are identical to their Japanese and Chinese counterparts.

The Japanese have been farming this fleshy fungus for over 600 years. Today, a great many Japanese homes in the countryside have racks with shiitake logs stacked on them just outside the door. Sometimes the mushrooms are for private use, but more often they are a supplemental cash crop. In all Japan there are 67,000 commercial mushroom producers.

Stir-fried Shiitakes

Since the eating of meat is forbidden by the Buddhist religion, shiitakes play a major role in Zen monastery cooking. Their thick, fleshy caps make a wonderful meat substitute. This typical Zen preparation can be enjoyed as a vegetable course or as an accompaniment to rice. Or chill the shiitakes and slice them into tossed green salads.

Serves 4 to 6

    1 pound medium shiitakes
    2 tablespoons vegetable oil
    2 tablespoons sake rice wine
    2 tablespoons soy sauce
    1 tablespoon mirin, available in oriental food shops
    1 tablespoon sugar
      Pinch of salt
    ¼ teaspoon chopped dried hot red pepper (optional)

1. Wipe the mushrooms with a damp cloth or brush. Separate the stems from the caps and discard. Holding a sharp knife at a 45° angle, score the caps with 2 diagonal cuts.
2. Heat the oil in a medium skillet, add the mushrooms, and stir-fry over high heat for about 3 minutes. Sprinkle

the mushrooms with the sake, then add the soy sauce, mirin, sugar, and salt. Continue stir-frying until all the liquid has evaporated. Sprinkle the mushrooms with the hot peppers and serve.

Fried Crab and Shiitake "Strudel"

The Chinese have been forced for centuries to travel countless miles to seek new homes after national upheavals. Everywhere they have settled they have adapted the food of their host countries into their own cuisine. The world has been made richer for their culinary ingenuity. This recipe would be equally at home in China or Vienna.

Serves 6 as a first course

¼ pound fresh shiitakes
2 tablespoons unsalted butter
¾ pound cooked crabmeat
12 ounces cream cheese at room temperature
1 egg yolk, slightly beaten
1 teaspoon salt
¼ teaspoon finely ground pepper (preferably Szechuan)
12 egg roll wrappers, available in supermarkets and oriental food shops
Vegetable oil for deep-frying

DIPPING SAUCE
½ cup vegetable oil
1 teaspoon hot sesame oil
¼ cup ketchup
1 teaspoon Worcestershire sauce
1 tablespoon soy sauce
1 tablespoon lemon juice

3 tablespoons vinegar
3 tablespoons honey
1 teaspoon salt
1 medium onion, finely grated

1. Wipe the mushrooms with a damp cloth or brush. Remove the stems and discard. Coarsely chop the caps. Melt the butter in a small skillet, add the mushrooms, and sauté over moderate heat, shaking the pan and tossing, for 5 minutes. Remove the pan from the stove to cool.

2. In a food processor fitted with the metal blade, process the crabmeat for 1 minute. Add the mushrooms and pulse on and off 4 times. Cut the cream cheese into 1-inch cubes and add it and the egg yolk to the crabmeat/mushroom mixture. Sprinkle with salt and pepper, and process until thoroughly blended.

3. Place one egg roll wrapper on a lightly floured pastry board or counter top in front of you so that the edges of the wrapper are parallel with the edges of the pastry board. Take care not to break the wrappers. If you accidentally tear one, do not use it. Working from top to bottom, place 3 tablespoons of the crab mix in a single line down the center of the wrapper, leaving a 1½-inch space at each end. Fold the top edge and the bottom edge of the wrapper over the crab mix. Carefully fold the right side of the wrapper over to cover the crab mix. With your fingers, dampen the left side of the wrapper slightly and fold over the right. The water will help seal the wrapper. The finished product should look like an egg roll or blintz. Repeat this process with the remaining wrappers.

4. Combine the Dipping Sauce ingredients in a bowl and whisk until the honey is completely dissolved and the ingredients are thoroughly mixed. Set aside.

5. In a large skillet heat enough oil to deep-fry the "stru-

dels" until it begins to ripple. Fry the strudels until golden brown. Drain on several layers of paper towel. Serve hot with small bowls of dipping sauce on the side.

Tenderloin of Beef with Shiitakes

The versatile shiitake can be used in soups, sautéed and added to salads, grilled as a vegetable course and, of course, in most dishes where mushrooms are called for. This amazingly flavorful oriental version of the classic beef stroganoff is a delight served over fresh spinach pasta.

Serves 4 to 6

½ pound shiitake mushrooms
6 tablespoons unsalted butter
3 medium onions, finely chopped
1½ pounds beef tenderloin, cut into strips about 2 inches long, ½ inch wide and ½ inch thick
2 tablespoons all-purpose flour
1½ cups rich beef stock (page 190), warmed
¾ cup sour cream
¼ cup crème fraîche (page 194)
Salt and freshly ground black pepper to taste

1. Wipe the mushrooms with a damp cloth or brush. Cut off and discard the stems. Slice the caps thin and set aside.
2. Melt 3 tablespoons of the butter in a large skillet, add the onions, and sauté over moderately-high heat, stirring occasionally, until they are golden. Add the meat and toss for 3 minutes. The meat should be cooked on the outside but remain rare inside. Remove the onions and meat to a heated plate and keep warm.
3. Melt the remaining 3 tablespoons butter in the skillet,

add the mushrooms, and sauté over moderate heat, stirring occasionally, for 5 minutes. Sprinkle on the flour and stir to blend well. Slowly stir in the warm broth and simmer 2 minutes. Stir in the sour cream and crème fraîche and simmer 2 minutes longer or until the sauce has thickened slightly. Season to taste.

4.   Return the meat and onions to the skillet and toss to coat with the sauce. Serve immediately.

Geza's Goulash

This dish was suggested to me by a dear friend who has the distinction of being, in my estimation, one of the world's great nonprofessional chefs. Successful actor and photographer as well as dedicated cook and host, Charles Korvin, or Geza, as he is known to his friends, tells me that he prepares this mushroom goulash whenever his guests are vegetarians. Served with a crusty bread and tossed salad, this is a a delicious but slimming meal. Shiitake mushrooms are ideal in this dish because they stand up to long cooking.

Serves 4

   ¾ pound shiitake mushrooms
   3 tablespoons vegetable oil
   2 large onions, finely chopped
   3 garlic cloves, crushed
   1 teaspoon kosher salt
   1 pound new potatoes, washed but not peeled
   1 teaspoon caraway seeds
1½ tablespoons sweet paprika (preferably Hungarian)
   1 green bell pepper, washed, seeded, and cut into
      thin strips
   2 large tomatoes, peeled and quartered

1. Wipe the mushrooms clean with a damp cloth, remove the stems, and cut the caps into quarters. Set aside.

2. Heat the oil in a heavy-bottomed dutch oven or stew pot for which you have a cover, add the onions and garlic and cook over moderate heat, stirring occasionally, until the onions are golden. Add the mushrooms, sprinkle them with salt (the salt will draw out their liquid), and toss. Cover the pot and cook over moderately low heat for 10 minutes. Do not let the vegetables dry out. If necessary, add a few tablespoons of water.

3. Cut the potatoes into cubes about the size of the quartered mushroom caps. Add the potatoes and caraway seeds to the mushrooms, then sprinkle with the paprika and stir to coat all the vegetables well. Gently stir in the pepper strips and tomatoes, and add water or vegetable broth just to cover. Bring the liquid to a boil, lower the heat, cover, and simmer until the potatoes are tender, about 30 minutes. Correct seasoning and serve.

VARIATION: Fresh boletes or meadow mushrooms may be substituted for the shiitakes, but they will not be as "chewy."

MATSUTAKES

GENUS: *Armillaria*
SPECIES: *ponderosa*
COMMON NAME: White Matsutake (Eng.); Matsutake (Jap.)
MARKET AVAILABILITY: Late November and December; in California they are available into February

◇   ◇   ◇

The exciting matsutake has a white cap with light brown scales in the center. Its stalk is thick, and like the cap is fleshy and edible after being trimmed. The matsutake has a spicy fragrance something like a mixture of pine boughs and cinnamon and a pronounced flavor reminiscent of pine woods. Like the bolete, its flavor is robust.

The Japanese consider the matsutake, which appears in Japan in late fall, the nobility of the fungus world. In fact, hunting matsutakes used to be a royal pastime. In 1889 an English diplomat's wife wrote in her diary, "I was much amused . . . to hear that the Empress-Dowager was leaving Tokyo, and taking a journey of several hours' duration, so as to enjoy some good mushroom-hunting!" Our reporter tells us that mushroom hunting was always "considered as a kind of artistic sport" and that in "the hunting parties only one specimen is sought after, the *matsu-take,* which, as its name implies, grows among the splendid pine trees of the hills. The *matsu-take* has a strong pungent flavor; and the soil of some of the pine woods is so highly impregnated with the spawn, that a little of it put down in woods where no mushrooms grow will at once render the ground abundantly fruitful."

Alas, the pine woods of Japan are no longer abundantly fruitful and the Japanese, who pay anywhere from $40 to $60 per mushroom, are having to import these fragrant fungi from Korea and the United States. The matsutake can be found in the Pacific Northwest under a variety of conifers (Douglas firs, ponderosa pines, and the like) and usually appears in winter.

Grilled Matsutakes

One of the simplest ways of preparing this flavorful mushroom is also one of the best—roasting. In some areas in the Pacific Northwest matsutakes are simply roasted over open fires like marshmallows. Try roasting them over aromatic wood chips, but if that isn't possible, pan-grill them.

Serves 4 as a first course

8 large matsutake mushrooms
  Vegetable oil for brushing the mushrooms and grill

DIPPING SAUCE
  3 tablespoons soy sauce
  2 tablespoons water
  1 tablespoon mirin, available in oriental food shops
  1 teaspoon sugar
  ½ teaspoon grated fresh ginger
  2 green onions, white part only, minced very fine

1.   Wipe the mushrooms well with a damp cloth. Trim the bases of the stems and thickly slice the mushrooms from the caps through the stems.

2. Light the coals or wood chips in a hibachi or grill. When the fire has died down and the coals have turned white, oil the grill and both sides of the mushroom slices. Place the slices on the grill and cook lightly about 2 minutes on each side (less if the slices are thin).

3. Meanwhile combine the sauce ingredients and divide among 4 small dipping bowls. Serve the mushrooms with the sauce on the side.

VARIATION: This method also may be used to grill shiitakes.

Grilled Tuna Steaks with Matsutakes

Grilled fresh tuna steaks are delicious, but when accompanied by sautéed matsutakes they become exceptional. Use mesquite or pecan chips for your fire if available. Take care not to leave the fish on the fire too long as tuna dries out easily.

Serves 4

   5 large matsutake mushrooms
1½ tablespoons soy sauce
   1 tablespoon mirin, available in oriental food shops
   3 teaspoons dry white wine
   1 teaspoon sugar
   4 fresh tuna steaks, each about 1½ inches thick
   3 tablespoons safflower or sunflower seed oil
     Kosher salt and freshly ground pepper to taste
     Bunches of fresh dill or softened *wakame* (dried kelp) for garnish (optional)

1. Wipe the mushrooms with a damp cloth, trim the stems, and thinly slice both caps and stems. Set aside.
2. Combine the soy sauce, mirin, wine, and sugar in a small bowl and stir until the sugar is completely dissolved.
3. Put the tuna steaks in a shallow enameled or glass baking dish, prick them all over with a fork, pour the sauce over them, and marinate for 10 minutes, turning occasionally.
4. Drain the steaks and place them on a grill over hot coals or grill them in a well-seasoned, ridged cast-iron pan. Grill the steaks 5 to 7 minutes on each side or just until cooked through.
5. Meanwhile, heat the oil in a skillet. Add the mushrooms and toss. Cook them, stirring occasionally, until they are wilted. Remove from the heat and sprinkle with salt and pepper. Serve the steaks on a bed of fresh dill or softened *wakame* accompanied by a serving of mushrooms.

ENOKITAKES

GENUS: *Flammulina*
SPECIES: *velutipes*
COMMON NAMES: Winter mushroom, Pinhead mushroom (Eng.); Enokitake (Jap.)
MARKET AVAILABILITY: The cultivated variety are available all year round

◇   ◇   ◇

When found in the wild, enokitakes have reddish orange caps that are very slippery to the touch. Their flesh is thick and appears white to yellow in the mature specimens. They usually grow in clusters on living trees in late fall, winter, and very early spring. Enokitakes have also been found in the mountains, where the snow lasts late into the spring and early summer. This wild variety has been found throughout the United States and is considered a common edible, but so far wild enokitakes have not made their way to our food shops.

The cultivated variety, which we do find in shops, looks nothing like its wild cousin. The "enoki," as it is familiarly termed here, is a product of Japan. It is cultivated in long thin glass tubes that encourage it to grow a very long stem (3 to 4 inches) and only a very tiny cap. Its color, or rather lack of it, is also a result of the cultivation process. Japanese cooks value its pristine whiteness as a symbol of purity, but relegate its use to garnishes for soups or other dishes. To my knowledge, it's never used as a central ingredient in any dish.

There's some dispute about its flavor. Some say enokis taste like grapes, others say radishes. There's one indisputable fact about them, however, and that is that they must be crunchy. If they are limp or soggy, don't buy or eat them.

The Japanese package them in plastic bags in which they keep remarkably well for several days even after the package has been opened. To use them, cut the individual mushrooms from their thick common base and use them in salads, to add crunch to steamed vegetables, or as garnishes with sushi, sashimi, or soups.

Chilled Enoki-Strawberry Soup

This beautiful chilled fruit soup makes the perfect setting for the texture and pure whiteness of the mushrooms. It would be an appropriate offering in the most elegant spa cuisine.

Serves 4 to 6

16 enokitake mushrooms of varying lengths
 4 cups rich beef stock (page 190) or canned beef bouillon
 1 small carrot, scraped and thinly sliced
 1 inner stalk celery with leaves, chopped
½ small bay leaf
 1 teaspoon dried mint
 1 level tablespoon sugar
 2 cups California red burgundy wine
 1 quart very ripe fresh strawberries, washed and hulled, or a 20-ounce package of frozen unsweetened strawberries, thawed, drained, and liquid reserved

1. Holding a sharp knife at a 45° angle, make one diagonal slice through the base of each mushroom. Set them aside.

2. In a saucepan or stockpot, combine the bouillon, carrot, celery, bay leaf, mint, sugar, and wine. Bring to a boil, reduce heat to low, and simmer, partially covered, for 20 minutes. Cool the stock, strain through a fine sieve, and discard the vegetables.

3. In a blender jar or food processor fitted with a metal blade, combine the fresh strawberries and one cup of the stock. If using frozen strawberries, combine the thawed strawberries, their liquid, and 1 cup of the stock. Purée.

4. Mix together the purée and remaining stock and chill at least 2 hours. To serve, ladle soup into individual serving bowls. Gently float 4 mushrooms in the shape of a fan in each bowl.

Enoki Salad Mimosa

A simple salad mimosa takes on new interest when enokis are added.

Serves 6

   1 package enokitake mushrooms
   1 head garden or Boston lettuce, thoroughly washed and drained
   1 small head red lettuce, thoroughly washed and drained
   ½ of the yellow leaves of 1 head of curly endive

DRESSING

3 tablespoons rice vinegar or white wine vinegar
½ teaspoon sugar
¼ teaspoon salt
½ teaspoon Dijon mustard
6 tablespoons good-quality olive oil
2 hard-cooked eggs, whites and yolks separated

1. Carefully trim the mushrooms from their common base and trim and separate those mushrooms that require it. Set them aside.
2. Tear the lettuce leaves into bite-sized pieces and place in a large salad bowl. Trim the tough parts of the endive and tear the leaves if necessary. Add the enoki, toss, and refrigerate until needed.
3. Combine the vinegar, sugar, salt, and mustard in a small bowl. Stir with a wire whisk until the sugar and salt are completely dissolved. Add the olive oil a little at a time, stirring with the whisk between additions to blend completely. Set aside at room temperature.
4. Press the egg yolks through a sieve and set aside until needed. Repeat the process with the egg whites.
5. To assemble the salad, whisk the dressing to blend, then add 2 tablespoons to the salad. Toss and taste. Add more dressing, 2 tablespoons at a time, tossing and tasting until the salad is to your liking. Sprinkle the sieved whites over the salad and pile the sieved yolks in the center. Bring to the table and toss once before serving. Pass a pepper mill separately.

NOTE: You may substitute your favorite dressing for the one suggested here.

DRIED
MUSHROOMS
for ALL SEASONS

Drying is the time-honored and most frequently used method of preserving mushrooms. In China dried mushrooms play important medical and religious roles. The Chinese use dried mushrooms as offerings at ancestral tombs, where fresh offerings are prohibited. Furthermore, dried fungi of all sorts have always been central ingredients in Chinese and Japanese traditional medicine.

In eighteenth century England urban families repairing to the country for the summer took with them supplies of morels and truffles, as well as ginger, nutmeg, and other such spices, which they considered essential for the good life. The morels they carried with them could only have been dried, and were most likely imported from France.

Today, in our own country, most dried mushrooms are also imported. Depending on the variety, they come from Japan, France, Italy, or Poland. However, there is a small but growing number of American commercial establishments that are drying (and canning) chanterelles, and who may expand into other varieties if the market warrants.

Always store dried mushrooms in tightly covered containers to maintain their flavor, and keep the containers in a dry place. Dampness is the arch enemy of dried mushrooms.

For use in most recipes dried mushrooms need to be reconstituted. To reconstitute dried mushrooms, simply soak them in warm (not hot) water to cover, for a period of between 15 and 30 minutes. The water in which they have been soaked should be strained (preferably through a paper coffee filter or several layers of absorbent paper towel) and saved, since it is full of mushroom flavor that can be added to sauces and soups at some other time. My favorite way of saving this precious liquor is simply to freeze it in an ice cube tray. When it is thoroughly frozen, I turn the cubes into a plastic bag, squeeze as much air as possible out of it, close it tightly, and put it back in the freezer. Then when I want to add a little flavor to any dish, I simply add a "mushroom cube" to the pan during the cooking process. You may choose to keep the various mushroom soaking liquids separately, or you might decide to combine them.

Some recipes for sauces, stews, or soups, may specify that you add the dried mushrooms directly to the pan. For such dishes, the mushrooms should first be washed under cold running water to remove as much sand and grit as possible.

One ounce of dried mushrooms is equal to approximately seven to ten ounces of reconstituted ones. Dried mushrooms have a tendency to be slightly rubbery, but in most cases, this minor drawback is more than compensated for by the heightened flavor they add to a dish.

◇   ◇   ◇

DRIED BOLETES

These can be found in most fine food stores packaged in small cellophane bags or in supermarkets in small plastic containers labeled "imported." Look for this mushroom especially in shops in Italian and Polish neighborhoods.

The bolete *(Boletus edulis)* is probably the most popular dried wild mushroom used in occidental cooking. Those sold in American shops are imported from France as cèpes, from Italy as porcini, and from Poland as "imported mushrooms." Some people feel that the cèpes and porcini are tastier than those from Poland; however, since their prices are generally higher, they tend to be carried in fewer shops than the "imported mushrooms." In fact, the difference in taste can be accounted for by the fact that "imported mushrooms" may contain several species of *Boletus,* whereas both the cepes and porcini are supposed to be only the species *edulis.*

Dried boletes are the most economical flavoring mushroom we can use. The deep, rich flavor of fresh boletes is intensified a hundredfold by drying. When used for flavoring a very little goes a long way.

Boletes are sometimes available canned in brine, but they are expensive, and lack flavor. I do not recommend their use.

To reconstitute dried boletes, put them in a strainer and put the strainer in a larger bowl. Pour hot, not boiling, water over them to cover. Let them soak 15 to 20 minutes unless the recipe instructs otherwise. Remove the strainer from the bowl and run cold water over the reconstituted mushrooms to loosen any sand that may still adhere. Drain and pat dry. Strain the soaking liquid through a paper coffee filter and save it for use in stock or soup.

The Romagnolis' Pasta with Porcini and Tomato Sauce

The Romagnolis, Margaret and Franco, have delighted the food-conscious public for many years with their many cookbooks and their very popular public television series, "The Romagnolis' Table." Through their elegant dishes and presentations they proved that there is more to la cucina Italiana than checkered tableclothes and candle-dripped Chianti bottles. In the Boston area, where they make their home, they are also known as hospitable restaurateurs who first introduced the joy of fresh pasta to thousands of grateful people. Here is their recipe for a hearty "evening with friends" dinner.

Serves 4 to 6 as a main dish

FOR THE SAUCE
1 ounce dried porcini (boletes), or 6 ounces fresh
2 cups plum tomatoes
4 tablespoons unsalted butter
4 tablespoons olive oil
½ carrot, minced
½ celery stalk, minced

1 heaping tablespoon minced onion
½ teaspoon dried basil, or 5 leaves fresh
   Freshly ground black pepper to taste
½ teaspoon salt or to taste

1.   Soak the dried porcini in warm water to cover 5 to 10 minutes or until softened.
2.   If using fresh tomatoes, skin them and chop them into small chunks. Do not purée them. If using canned tomatoes chop them coarsely then rub them through a sieve to remove the seeds. Set aside.
3.   Melt the butter in a large sauté pan and add the olive oil. Add the minced vegetables and basil and sauté until the vegetables are limp and golden, about 3 minutes. Add the sieved or processed tomatoes, bring to a boil, lower the heat, and simmer about 15 minutes, uncovered.
4.   Lift the softened porcini from their soaking liquid, rinse, drain, and pat them dry. Cut the mushrooms into ¼-inch-wide strips where possible and add them to the thickened sauce. Simmer about 5 minutes longer, add salt and pepper to taste, and then serve on cooked, drained pasta.
5.   If you are using fresh porcini, wipe them clean, cut them into ¼-inch slices, and add them to the sauce when it has been on the heat for about 10 minutes. Continue cooking about 10 minutes more or until the mushrooms are cooked and the sauce has been reduced a bit and coats a wooden spoon. Serve as above.
NOTE: Tomatoes may be canned or fresh, but we do not advise using those put up in tomato purée.

◇   ◇   ◇

FOR THE PASTA
  4 to 5 quarts water
  1 teaspoon salt per quart of water
  14 ounces fettucine, packaged or homemade

  Bring the water to a boil. Add the salt and the pasta, cover, and bring back to a boil. Uncover the pot and boil according to the suggested time on the pasta box. (Handmade pasta cooks in about 3 minutes if fresh.) Taste your pasta about 2 minutes before suggested cooking time is up and when it is cooked but still has a bite to it, it is done. Drain and add sauce.

Spa Risotto
(RISOTTO LEGGÉRO)

The traditional risotto con funghi is made with butter, beef marrow, and boletes, but in this health-conscious age we have learned to limit the butter and eliminate the beef marrow. Here is my adaptation of this great Italian classic.

Serves 6

  2 ounces dried boletes, reconstituted
  4 tablespoons virgin olive oil
  1 small onion, finely chopped
  2 cups Arborio rice
  ½ cup white wine
  5 cups rich chicken stock (page 192) or canned chicken, mixed with the strained mushroom liquid
  2 or 3 strands of saffron softened in 1 tablespoon water

Salt and freshly ground black pepper to taste

2 tablespoons unsalted butter, cut into small cubes

½ cup freshly grated Parmesan cheese (preferably imported)

1.   Using a strainer or a slotted spoon, remove the mushrooms from the warm water, then rinse them under cold water to remove any sand that has not been loosened. Pat dry and chop coarse.

2.   Heat the oil in a large nonstick skillet for which you have a tight cover. Add the onion and sauté over moderate heat until it begins to color. Add the rice and toss to coat completely. Add the mushrooms and the wine and mix. Cook until the wine is completely absorbed. (This will take only a few minutes.) Pour in the broth, saffron, and saffron soaking liquid and bring to a boil. Reduce the heat, cover, and cook over low heat until all the broth is absorbed, about 20 to 30 minutes.

3.   Test the rice occasionally by pinching it between your thumb and forefinger. It should be al dente, not soft. If the rice is done before all the liquid in the pan has been absorbed, simply turn it out into a strainer and drain. If the liquid has been completely absorbed before the rice is tender, add additional hot broth and continue cooking.

4.   To serve, place the cooked rice in a large heated serving bowl and correct the seasoning. Add the butter and 2 tablespoons of cheese. Toss until the butter is melted and serve immediately. Pass the remaining cheese separately.

◇   ◇   ◇

Grandma's Dumplings

Dried boletes were a staple in my grandmother's kitchen, so it seems only natural that I should offer this adaptation of her famous mushroom dumplings. These dumplings are particularly delicious served with a sauce made from mushroom soaking liquid.

Serves 4 to 6

  3 tablespoons rendered chicken fat at room
    temperature
½ ounce dried boletes, reconstituted and chopped fine
  1 teaspoon grated onion
  6 eggs, separated
  1 teaspoon salt
⅛ teaspoon freshly ground black pepper
  1 cup, coarse, dried bread crumbs

1.   Heat 1 tablespoon of the fat in a small nonstick skillet, add the mushrooms and onion, and cook over moderate heat 3 minutes, stirring. Remove vegetables to a bowl and let them cool completely. Discard the fat remaining in the pan.

2.   Beat the egg whites until stiff. Set aside.

3.   Using an electric mixer, beat the yolks until they are a pale yellow (about 7 to 12 minutes). Add the mushrooms, salt, and pepper and mix thoroughly. Gently fold this mixture into the beaten egg whites. Then fold in the bread crumbs, 1 tablespoon at a time. Refrigerate for 1 hour.

4.   Bring 4 quarts of salted water to a rapid boil. While the water is coming to a boil, wet your hands and form the chilled batter into 12 equal balls. Drop the balls into the

boiling water, reduce the heat, cover, and cook the dumplings slowly for about 30 minutes. Remove them from the water with a slotted spoon, drain, and serve, either plain or with the sauce.

THE SAUCE

Makes about ¾ cup

> 1 cup mushroom soaking liquid
> 1½ tablespoons butter
> 1 tablespoon all-purpose flour
> Salt and pepper to taste

1.   Heat the mushroom soaking liquid in a small saucepan (if you do not have 1 cup of liquid, make up the difference with canned beef bouillon or dry red wine). Set aside and keep warm.
2.   Melt the butter in a small nonstick saucepan over low heat. Sprinkle the butter with the flour and stir to blend completely. Slowly add the liquid, stirring continuously, until well blended. Raise the heat to moderate and cook the sauce, stirring occasionally, until thickened. Season to taste with salt and pepper, pour over the dumplings and serve.

◇ ◇ ◇

DRIED CHANTERELLES

Freeze-dried chanterelles can now be purchased all year round, thanks to various mushrooming firms in Canada and Oregon. When reconstituted they have almost the same chewy texture as the fresh, but unfortunately sometimes lack their full flavor. Nevertheless, they are a lovely substitute when you feel you want chanterelles.

Reconstitute these freeze-dried mushrooms in the same manner as boletes (page 168). Like boletes, they should yield from seven to ten times their dry weight. However, one Canadian firm claims that the freeze-drying process produces yields of 14 times their dry weight, which makes their product relatively economically priced.

Herbed Chanterelles

If you have a little pot of marjoram growing on your windowsill, you might like to try this flavorful dish. It makes a delightful first course, and is wonderfully easy to prepare. Serve it hot or at room temperature.

2½ ounces dried chanterelles, reconstituted in water
2 tablespoons olive oil
1 small onion, minced
1 clove garlic, minced
1 tablespoon chopped fresh marjoram or 1 teaspoon dried
¾ cup sour cream
Salt and pepper to taste
Finely shredded red cabbage
1 tablespoon chopped parsley

1.   Remove the chanterelles from their soaking liquid, rinse under cold water, drain, and pat dry. Slice lengthwise and reserve.

2.   Heat the oil in a heavy-bottomed 1-quart saucepan, add the onion, and cook over moderate heat, stirring, until it begins to color. Lower the heat and add the garlic and mushroom slices and cook 4 minutes or until the mushrooms give up their liquid. Sprinkle the mushrooms with the marjoram, cover, and cook an additional 8 minutes, stirring occasionally. If the vegetables begin to look dry, add a tablespoon of soaking liquid and continue cooking. Stir in the sour cream and continue cooking an additional 2 minutes. Do not let the cream boil. Taste and add salt and pepper if desired.

3.   To serve, arrange a bed of shredded cabbage on each serving plate and spoon the mushrooms over it. Sprinkle with parsley and serve.

◇   ◇   ◇

Chanterelles Hunter's Style

(Pfifferling Jäger Art)

In Europe no chic picnic or al fresco outing would be complete without an array of pickles. My favorite is the following pickled chanterelle dish.

Serves 4

2 ounces dried small chanterelles, reconstituted
2 tablespoons cider vinegar
½ teaspoon sugar
2 tablespoons safflower or sunflower seed oil
2 tablespoons chopped cornichon or dilled pickle
2 tablespoons chopped pimientos
½ tablespoon finely chopped sun-dried tomato
½ cup cooked peas, fresh or frozen
⅛ teaspoon dried tarragon, crushed
  Salt and freshly ground black pepper to taste

1. Remove the mushrooms from their soaking liquid, rinse under cold water, drain, and pat dry. If the chanterelles are large, cut them into quarters; if small, leave them whole.
2. Combine the vinegar and sugar in a small bowl and stir until the sugar is completely dissolved. Set aside.
3. Heat the oil in a small heavy-bottomed skillet and add the mushrooms. Sauté them, stirring, 4 to 5 minutes. Add the seasoned vinegar and cook 1 minute longer. Remove from the heat.
4. Combine the remaining ingredients in a small bowl. Turn the mushrooms and their marinade into the bowl, and toss. Season with salt and pepper to taste, cover, and chill at least 2 hours before serving.

◇　◇　◇

DRIED MORELS

If boletes are the most popular dried mushrooms in Western use, morels certainly follow close behind. The very distinctive flavor of this mushroom is considerably intensified by drying; some people actually prefer the taste of dried morels to that of the fresh.

Only very small morels are customarily dried, so use them primarily for flavoring and texture. Since they are often torn before drying and tear easily after soaking, they are not suitable for stuffing.

Morels should be washed in several changes of cold water even before soaking because their honeycombed cap may be hiding a good bit of sand. Soften them in warm water, as suggested for boletes (page 168).

◇　◇　◇

Morels with Summer Vegetables

Color, texture, and flavor combine in this vegetable dish to produce a lovely companion to poached or steamed fish.

Serves 4

1½ ounces dried morels, reconstituted
  3 medium-sized sweet red peppers
  6 small or 4 large (approximately 8-inch) zucchini
  4 tablespoons extra virgin olive oil
  1 tablespoon minced shallots
  1 small clove garlic, minced
  1 tablespoon balsamic vinegar
 ¼ teaspoon sugar
   Kosher salt and freshly ground black pepper to taste

1. Remove the morels from their soaking liquid, pat dry, and cut lengthwise in quarters. Set aside.
2. Roast the peppers under a broiler or on an open flame until the skin is charred all over. Place the roasted peppers in a paper bag for 5 to 10 minutes, remove, and peel them. Remove the stem, seeds, and ribs and cut into 2-inch-long matchstick slices. Set aside.
3. Wash the zucchini, trim both ends, and cut the zucchini into 2-inch lengths. Slice each of these 4 times lengthwise, then cut each of these slices into matchstick width slices. Set them in a colander and sprinkle with a little salt. Let them drain 3 or 4 minutes, then pat dry. Set aside.
4. Heat the oil in a large nonstick skillet, add the shallots, and sauté until golden. Add the morels, toss to coat, and cook, stirring, for 2 minutes. Add the garlic, peppers, and zucchini and cook, stirring occasionally, 5 minutes.

5. Combine the vinegar and sugar in a small bowl and stir until the sugar is completely dissolved. Add this to the vegetables in the pan and stir to mix. Raise the heat and cook, stirring, 2 to 3 minutes longer or until the liquid in the pan is completely absorbed.

Zucchini Stuffed with Morels

This dish has long been a family favorite at our house. Don't let the long list of ingredients discourage you; the actual work involved is minimal.

Serves 4

1 ounce dried morels, reconstituted
2 tablespoons unsalted butter
2 large shallots, minced
1 package frozen peas, cooked
2 tablespoons sour cream
   Generous pinch cayenne
   Generous pinch nutmeg
   Generous pinch dried thyme, crushed
¼ cup chopped cashew or macadamia nuts
4 medium zucchini, cut in half lengthwise and
   sprinkled with a little salt
½ cup very dry white wine
1 tablespoon vegetable oil
1 teaspoon salt
   Freshly ground black pepper
1 small bay leaf
2 generous tablespoons freshly grated Parmesan cheese
   (preferably imported)

—— 179 ——

1.   Remove the morels from their soaking liquid and pat dry. Chop coarse and reserve.

2.   In a small nonstick skillet, melt the butter, add the shallots, and sauté over moderate heat until they begin to take on color. Add the mushrooms and toss to coat. Reduce the heat, cover, and cook 5 minutes. Turn the vegetables and any liquid that remains in the pan into a mixing bowl. Set aside.

3.   Purée the peas and the sour cream in a blender or a food processor fitted with a metal blade. Add the purée to the mushrooms and stir to mix. Stir in the cayenne, nutmeg, thyme, and nuts. Set aside.

4.   Preheat the oven to 400°.

5.   Using a melon ball cutter or a teaspoon, scoop out the center portion of each zucchini half, leaving it ready for stuffing. Avoid breaking through the skin.

6.   In a nonstick skillet just large enough to hold all the zucchini halves in one layer, combine the wine, oil, salt, pepper (about 2 twists of the mill) and bay leaf, bring to a boil, and cook 30 seconds. Place the zucchini halves, cut side down, in the liquid and add water to cover. Bring the liquid back to a boil and boil 2 minutes. Remove the zucchini halves and drain, cut side down, on several layers of paper towel, until they are cool enough to handle.

7.   Stuff each half with the morel/pea stuffing, sprinkle with some cheese, and bake for 10 minutes or until the cheese is golden. Serve immediately.

◇   ◇   ◇

DRIED SHIITAKES

Small shiitakes can be found packaged in the "international food" section of most supermarkets, but for larger, more satisfying specimens look in oriental or gourmet shops.

In China and Japan the traditional way of drying mushrooms is near a wood fire. This imparts a slight but unmistakable smoky flavor to the dried mushroom. It is this smokiness combined with the mushroom's meaty flavor that cooks prize in dried shiitakes.

Small, dark, dried shiitakes are used extensively in Chinese cuisine, especially in braised and stir-fried dishes, because their smoky taste and chewy texture stand up exceptionally well to high heat and lengthy cooking. Furthermore, their flavor doesn't yield to the hot peppers of Szechuan and Mongol cooking nor the competitive flavors, in Japanese cuisine, of dried bonito and sea vegetables. The Japanese prefer large specimens with rusty brown cracked caps (the *Han Doko* type).

To reconstitute dried shiitakes, soak them in warm water for a minimum of 15 minutes. Drain them and strain the soaking liquid as described previously to save for future use. Gently pat the mushrooms dry, cut off the stems and discard them. The caps are now ready to be cooked.

Stir-fried Rainbow Vegetables in a Spicy Ginger-Garlic Sauce

Nina Simonds is one of this country's leading and most enthusiastic exponents of Chinese cuisine. Her articles and cookbooks on the subject are always innovative, authentic, and exciting. This recipe is an example of the interesting flavors that result from the use of dried and fresh shiitakes in combination.

Serves 6

6 dried black mushrooms, softened in hot water for 15 minutes
2 medium-sized yellow or red peppers, rinsed, cored, and seeded
½ pound fresh snow peas, ends snapped and veiny strings removed

SEASONINGS
1 tablespoon minced gingerroot
1 tablespoon minced garlic

SAUCE
3 tablespoons soy sauce
1 tablespoon sugar
1 tablespoon plus ½ teaspoon sesame oil

REMAINING INGREDIENTS
1½ tablespoons rice wine
1 cup very thinly sliced fresh shiitakes, caps only
1 cup 1-inch lengths Chinese garlic chives, or scallion greens
1½ tablespoons safflower or corn oil

1. Remove and discard the stems from the dried mushrooms and finely shred the caps. Cut the peppers lengthwise into matchstick-size shreds. Rinse the snow peas. Prepare the seasonings. Make the sauce by thoroughly mixing the soy sauce, sugar, and ½ teaspoon sesame oil together until the sugar is completely dissolved. Have the rice wine, fresh shiitakes, and garlic chives or scallion greens in readiness.

2. Heat a wok and add the safflower or corn oil and the remaining 1 tablespoon sesame oil. Heat until the oil is near smoking, then add the seasonings and dried black mushrooms. Stir-fry about 10 to 15 seconds, until fragrant, then add the peppers and snow peas. Toss lightly over high heat, stirring constantly. Add the rice wine. Continue cooking for about 1 minute. Add the fresh shiitakes and garlic chives or scallions and continue cooking for another 30 seconds. Add the sauce. Toss lightly over high heat for an additional 10 seconds to coat thoroughly and remove to a serving platter. Serve warm or at room temperature.

NOTE: For additional spiciness, you may add ½ teaspoon hot chili paste to the seasoning mixture.

◇   ◇   ◇

Peking Chicken and Mushrooms

On a recent trip to China, my husband and I were treated to a lovely baked chicken smothered in mushrooms and onions. The dish, which could easily be a variation of grandmother's chicken and mushroom "Saturday supper," is in fact an ancient Peking specialty, proving once again the universality of good food.

Serves 6

8 dried shiitake mushrooms, reconstituted
1 large onion, trimmed and peeled
4 tablespoons safflower or sunflower seed oil
6 chicken legs and thighs, separated
1 teaspoon coarse salt
¼ teaspoon freshly ground pepper, preferably Szechuan

SAUCE
½ teaspoon sugar
1 tablespoon whiskey
2 tablespoons soy sauce

GARNISH
2 tablespoons chopped fresh coriander (optional)

1. Preheat the oven to 375°.
2. Drain the mushrooms and pat dry. Cut off and discard the stems. Cut the caps into medium-sized slices and set aside.
2. Place the onion on a cutting board. Using a sharp knife and cutting from the top down, but not all the way through, cut the onion into sixteenths. Pull each section from the root end and then separate its layers. Set aside.
3. Rub 2 tablespoons of the oil over the chicken pieces.

Sprinkle the meat with salt and pepper and place the chicken pieces in a shallow baking pan and bake for 45 to 50 minutes, or until both sides are crisp and brown and the chicken is completely cooked.

4.   To prepare the sauce, dissolve the sugar in the whiskey and soy sauce. Set aside.

5.   A few minutes before the chicken is done, heat the remaining 2 tablespoons oil in a wok or large skillet. Add the onion and stir-fry for 1 minute. Add the mushroom slices and continue stir-frying for 3 additional minutes. Add the sauce to the wok. Toss and cook, stirring, 30 seconds. Arrange the chicken pieces on an attractive serving platter. Spoon the vegetables over them, and sprinkle with the chopped coriander. Serve immediately.

DRIED WOOD EARS

This dark brown fungus, which when fresh resembles a human ear and when dry looks like pieces of crushed brown paper, is used extensively in Chinese cooking and sometimes in dishes of Southeast Asia. It adds no flavor, but its firm, gelatinous texture provides a desirable contrast to some otherwise velvety foods.

Recent medical research indicates that this fungus, which the Chinese, who call it *mo-er,* have long associated with longevity, has in it a substance that tends to thin the blood. Some researchers think that eating wood ears with garlic and scallions, as is often done in China, may explain the low incidence of atherosclerotic diseases there.

Chinese cooks may not know of the scientific research going on around one of their favorite ingredients, but they will all tell you that drinking a tea made from *mo-er* will ease a headache, is good for stomach ailments, and leads to a long and happy life.

Wood ears require long soaking—a minimum of 30 minutes—in hot water. If any tough parts remain after soaking simply trim them and discard. Discard the soaking liquid as well.

Stir-fried Tofu with Wood Ears and Shiitakes

This simple stir-fry dish will surely become a "quick dinner" favorite.

Serves 4 to 6

SAUCE
1½ teaspoons sugar
  2 tablespoons soy sauce
  2 tablespoons dry white wine

  6 wood ears, reconstituted
  6 small dried shiitakes, reconstituted
  1 clove garlic, minced
  6 ounces very lean ground pork
  2 tablespoons vegetable oil
  1 piece of fresh gingerroot the size of a quarter, peeled and cut into thin strips
  1 medium carrot, scraped and cut into 2-inch julienne strips
  1 block firm tofu, coarsely mashed
  2 scallions, white and green parts, trimmed and cut on the diagonal into ½-inch lengths
  1 egg, beaten

1. Stir sauce ingredients, together in a small bowl until sugar dissolves.

2. Remove the wood ears from the soaking liquid, trim away any tough parts if necessary, pat dry, and cut into ¼-inch slices. Drain the shiitakes and cut off and discard the stems. Cut each cap into 8 slices. Combine with the wood ears and reserve.

3.   Using your hands, mix the garlic and pork thoroughly. Set aside.

4.   Heat the oil in a well-seasoned wok, and add the ginger and the seasoned pork. Keep mashing the pork with a wooden spoon to make sure all the meat gets cooked and no lumps remain. After the meat has lost all of its pink color, continue cooking, stirring, 2 minutes longer.

5.   Add the mushrooms and carrot and cook 3 minutes or until the carrot is tender. Stir in the tofu and cook until heated through. Pour the sauce over all the ingredients, add the scallions, and mix well. Cook, stirring, 30 seconds. Stir in the egg and remove the wok from the heat. When the egg is cooked, serve with boiled rice.

Fragrant Steamed Bass

The Chinese have turned steamed fish into an art form. Serve this exquisite dish on a bed of seaweed and create your own masterpiece.

Serves 4 to 6

   6 wood ears, reconstituted
3/4 teaspoon grated fresh gingerroot
   2 star anise
1/2 teaspoon coarse salt
   1 tablespoon soy sauce
   1 tablespoon dry sherry
   2 teaspoons vegetable oil
   1 teaspoon sesame seed oil
   2 scallions, white and green parts, trimmed, and cut
      into 1½-inch diagonal slices
   1 whole dressed sea bass weighing about 2 to 3
      pounds, washed and dried inside and out

1.   Drain the wood ears and trim away any tough parts if necessary. Cut them into ¼-inch slices and reserve.

2.   In a small bowl, combine the ginger, anise, salt, soy sauce, sherry, and oils and stir until the salt is completely dissolved. Stir in the mushrooms and scallions and let stand at room temperature for 5 minutes.

3.   Arrange the fish on a heatproof platter and make three shallow diagonal cuts across the body. Place a steaming rack in a deep pan or steamer large enough to hold the fish. Fill the pan with water just 1 inch below the top of the rack and bring the water to a soft boil. Place the fish on its platter on the rack. Pour the sauce over the fish, cover the pan, and lower the heat. Steam the fish over softly boiling water for 12 minutes, or until done. Remove the star anise and serve.

◇   ◇   ◇

BASIC RECIPES

These basic recipes are included for those who hold strongly to the belief that "there is nothing like home-made." However, there are many good quality commercial products that may be substituted for these items and you should feel free to use them if you prefer.

Beef Stock

There are many good canned commercial stocks available, but home-made stocks are something special.

Makes 7 cups

2½ pounds beef bones cut to expose the marrow
  2 pounds veal knuckle bones, cut like the beef (see Note)
  2 large carrots, chopped
  1 medium turnip, chopped
  2 leeks white and green parts, washed, trimmed, and chopped
  1 stalk celery, chopped
  1 cup loosely packed celery leaves, chopped

2 medium onions, quartered
2 cloves garlic, unpeeled
3 tablespoons tomato paste
3 whole cloves
8 black peppercorns
1 sprig fresh tarragon or ½ teaspoon dried
1 tablespoon fresh thyme, leaves only, or 1 teaspoon dried
1 large or 2 small bay leaves
2 tablespoons kosher salt
2 teaspoons sugar
6 quarts water

1.   Preheat the oven to 425°.
2.   Place the bones in one layer in a large deep rectangular baking pan (such as a lasagna pan); do not let them touch. Bake in the preheated oven for 30 minutes. Spread the carrots, turnip, leeks, celery, and celery leaves over the bottom of the pan around the bones, then turn the bones over onto the vegetables and bake an additional 30 minutes. The vegetables should not brown.
3.   Turn the bones and vegetables into a large stockpot, add the remaining ingredients, including the water, and bring rapidly to a boil. Immediately reduce the heat to low and simmer the stock, uncovered, for 4 hours. Do not allow the stock to boil. Carefully skim and discard the foam as it forms on the surface of the stock.
4.   Remove the bones and discard. Line a large sieve with 4 layers of cheese cloth or heavy muslin and strain the stock through it. Discard the vegetables, correct the seasoning and chill the stock in the refrigerator until the fat has risen to the top and solidified. Remove the fat and discard it.

5.   Return the stock to the pot and bring it to a simmer over moderate heat. Continue to simmer it 30 minutes longer. Cool it slightly, place the stock in measured containers and refrigerate for up to a week or freeze until needed.

NOTE: You will probably have to order veal bones from your butcher ahead of time. If they are unavailable, use beef bones. Try to find bones that still have meat on them or add some stew meat to the bones. The more meat you have the richer the stock will be.

Chicken Stock

Makes approximately 8 cups

    4 pounds chicken wings and backs
    2 tablespoons vegetable oil
    2 large carrots, coarsely chopped
    1 large onion, coarsely chopped
    1 cup coarsely chopped celery with leaves
    2 large parsnips, coarsely chopped
    1 medium can tomatoes with their juice
    1 large sweet potato, peeled and cut into 6 pieces
    4 sprigs flat leaf parsley
    1 large bay leaf
    1 garlic clove, unpeeled
  ½ teaspoon dried marjoram
  ¼ teaspoon dried savory
1½ tablespoons kosher salt
    5 whole peppercorns
    2 teaspoons sugar
    6 quarts water

1.   Lightly brown the chicken parts in the oil in the bottom of a large stockpot. Add the carrots, onions, and celery and stir to mix. Cook, stirring occasionally, until the vegetables begin to soften, about 5 minutes. Do not let them brown. Add the remaining ingredients and bring rapidly to a boil.

2.   Reduce the heat immediately to moderate and simmer the stock uncovered for 4 hours. Skim and discard the foam as it appears on the surface of the stock.

3.   Line a large sieve with 4 layers of cheesecloth or 1 layer of heavy muslin. Strain the stock through the sieve and discard the solids. Let the stock cool slightly.

4.   Place the stock in the refrigerator until all the fat has risen to the top and solidified. Remove the fat and discard it.

5.   Return the defatted chicken stock to the pot, taste and correct seasoning. Return the stock to a simmer over moderate heat. Continue simmering the stock for 30 minutes. Taste again and correct seasoning if necessary. Cool, transfer to measured containers, and refrigerate for up to 5 days or freeze until needed.

◇   ◇   ◇

Crème Fraîche

This recipe uses a good deal more buttermilk than is usually suggested but it guarantees a thick product. If you prefer thinner cream let it stand 48 hours. If you like your cream thick let it stand 72 hours. If you prefer your cream sweeter, use only 3 tablespoons buttermilk.

Makes 2 cups

1 pint heavy cream
4 tablespoons whole milk buttermilk

1.   Combine the cream and buttermilk in a screwtop jar. Cover it tightly and shake vigorously for 1 minute.
2.   Set the jar aside in a warm (not hot) place for 48 to 72 hours. If the cream is too cold it will not thicken. Heat, on the other hand, will kill the culture. The longer the cream remains outside the refrigerator, the thicker it will become and with practice you will be able to produce the thickness of cream you prefer. Crème fraîche should never be thinner than commercial sour cream. When it is to your liking, place the cream in the refrigerator. It will keep for 3 weeks.

◇   ◇   ◇

Pie Crust

Recipes for pie crust are remarkably alike. This one will give you a rich and flaky crust large enough for a two-crust pie or a two-crust 10-inch tarte.

Perhaps the reason most often pointed to for a failed crust is the use of too much water. After you have cut the shortening into the flour add only very small quantities of water, then work it quickly into the dough before you add more water. Use only the amount it takes to make the dough hold together in a ball. In making a pie crust it is very important to keep the ingredients cold, particularly if your kitchen is warm.

Makes enough dough for two 9-inch pie crusts or two 10-inch tart crusts.

2½ cups sifted all-purpose flour, chilled
1 teaspoon salt
8 tablespoons unsalted, butter, chilled
½ cup vegetable shortening, chilled
4 to 6 tablespoons ice water

1. Sift the flour and salt together into a large mixing bowl. Cut 4 tablespoons of butter and all the shortening into the flour using a pastry blender or two table knives. Be sure to incorporate the flour at the bottom of the bowl.
2. When the flour and shortening mixture is the consistency of corn meal, add the remaining butter and cut it in until the mixture resembles small peas. Toss once or twice with a fork then sprinkle 4 tablespoons of ice water, 1 tablespoon at a time, over the flour, tossing with a fork after each addition.
3. Press the moistened pastry together and remove from the bowl that portion that easily sticks together. If any

flour/shortening mixture remains in the bowl continue to add 1 teaspoon of water at a time, tossing between additions, until the dough holds together when pressed. (Too much water makes the dough tough and too little will cause it to crack when it bakes, so it is important to get the right balance.) Add it to the rest of the dough.

4. To make a two-crust pie, Form the dough into 2 balls, one using ⅔ of the dough the other the remaining ⅓. Wrap each ball in wax paper and chill at least 2 hours or preferably overnight.

5. To form the crust, sprinkle a pastry cloth, or board covered with a coarse linen towel, lightly with flour and rub it in. Insert your rolling pin into a cloth "stocking" (available in cookware shops) and dust the cloth lightly with flour. Flatten the larger ball of dough with the heel of your hand and roll the dough out quickly but lightly, starting from the center and working outward. Heavy pressure on the rolling pin may result in the dough sticking and possibly breaking so use a light touch. Roll out the dough to ⅛-inch thickness for the bottom crust. Gently lift and fold the dough in half and place it on half the pan. Unfold it and cover the other half of the pan, then press it in to line it as directed in your recipe.

6. Repeat this process with the smaller ball of dough but roll it out slightly thinner. Follow the directions in your recipe for forming the top crust and for baking.

NOTE: For a one-crust pie, cut the recipe in half, or divide the dough into two equal size balls. Freeze the second ball for later use.

◇ ◇ ◇

MAIL ORDER SOURCES *of* MUSHROOMS

American Spoon Foods
411 East Lake Street
Petoskey, Michigan 49770
(614) 347-9030
VARIETIES: morels, boletes
FORM: fresh, dried
CATALOG: free

Dean & DeLuca
121 Prince Street
New York, New York 10012

Epicurean Specialty
6817 California Street
San Francisco, California
94121
(415) 668-1843
VARIETIES: morels, boletes,
oysters, chanterelles, Oriental
species
FORM: dried
CATALOG: free

Flying Foods International
43-43 Ninth Street
Long Island City, New York
11101

H. Roth & Son
1577 First Avenue
New York, New York 10028

Il Conte di Savoia
555 West Roosevelt Road
Chicago, Illinois 60607

Jim Jamail & Sons Food
Market
3114 Kirby Drive
Houston, Texas 77098
(713) 523-5535
VARIETIES: European, Oriental
FORM: dried, canned, fresh

The Kinoko Company Ltd.
P.O. Box 14551
Oakland, California 94614
(415) 537-5909
VARIETIES: shiitake, wood ear,
medicinal fungi
FORM: dried
CATALOG: free

Kirsch Mushroom Co. Inc.
751 Drake Street
Bronx, New York 10474
(212) 991-4977
VARIETIES: boletes, morels,
Agaricus
FORM: dried, powdered,
kibbled

La Cuisine
323 Cameron Street
Alexandria, Virginia 22314
(703) 836-4435
VARIETIES: morels, boletes, etc.
FORM: dried
CATALOG: $3; also newsletter,
mushroom cookbooks

Le Jardin du Gourmet
West Danville, Vermont
05873
VARIETIES: chanterelles,
boletes, truffles, morels
FORM: canned, dried

Myco-Man
G. F. Vulker Inc.
P.O. Box 6310 Station F
Hamilton, Ontario L9C 6L9
Canada
(416) 387-6550
VARIETIES: chanterelles,
morels, boletes, etc.
FORM: dried
CATALOG: free

S. E. Rykoff & Co.
P.O. Box 21467, Market St.
Station
Los Angeles, California
90021-9998
(213) 622-4131
VARIETIES: European,
Oriental, Chilean
FORM: dried, canned
CATALOG: free

Todaro Bros.
557 2nd Avenue
New York, New York 10016
(212) 679-7766
VARIETIES: European truffles,
boletes, morels, chanterelles
FORM: fresh, dried
CATALOG: free

Vanilla, Saffron Imports
70 Manchester Street
San Francisco, California
94110
(415) 648-8990
VARIETIES: Mexican morels,
boletes, chanterelles, Spanish
truffles
FORM: dried
CATALOG: free

Western Biologicals Ltd.
P.O. Box 46466 Station G
Vancouver, British Columbia
V6R 4G7 Canada

(604) 226-0986
VARIETIES: native wild,
Oriental
FORM: fresh, dried
CATALOG: $2
Also supplies spawn, growing
equipment, live cultures

Williams-Sonoma
Mail Order Department
P.O. Box 7456
San Francisco, California
94120

INDEX

◊   ◊   ◊

ABOUT THE AUTHOR

Margaret Leibenstein's interest in food began when as a child she was allowed to stir the great cauldrons of chicken stock simmering in the kitchen of her grandparents' hotel in Quatla, Mexico. Since then, fine food, its history and preparation, have been the major preoccupations of her life.

Today, she is president of the Culinary Historians of Boston, past member of the Board of Directors of the Women's Culinary Guild of New England, and member of the American Institute of Wine and Food and the International Association of Cooking Professionals. She has taught gourmet cooking privately, at the prestigious Cambridge Center for Adult Education and on several television programs, including Dr. Timothy Johnson's "Health Beat." Her articles on food appear in a variety of newspapers and food magazines.

As the wife of Harvard University Economist Harvey Leibenstein she has travelled extensively, studying and practicing her art in most countries of Europe as well as in Scandinavia, Latin America, the Middle East, and Asia. This is her third cookbook.